SPEAKING
OF MY LIFE

SPEAKING OF MY LIFE

The Art of Living in the Cultural Revolution

EDITED BY
JACOB NEEDLEMAN

PUBLISHED IN SAN FRANCISCO BY
HARPER & ROW, PUBLISHERS
NEW YORK, HAGERSTOWN, SAN FRANCISCO, LONDON

FIRST EDITION
Designed by Leigh McLellan

Library of Congress Cataloging in Publication Data
Main entry under title:

Speaking of my life.

    1. Conduct of life—Addresses, essays, lectures.
I. Needleman, Jacob.
BJ1581.2.S64   1979   170'.202   78–19502
ISBN 0–06–250643–9

79 80 81 82 83 10 9 8 7 6 5 4 3 2 1

Contents

Preface

WHEN THE INDUSTRIAL revolution threatened to lower human values in nineteenth century England, artists like William Blake, Ruskin and William Morris spoke up, showing sensible ways to direct the social effects positively. Today, the quality of our lives is imperilled by a burgeoning technology and there is deep uncertainty about what this is doing to us; whether to move towards it or run as far away as possible. Considering how quickly technology spreads, invading every aspect of our lives, it cannot be treated as a joke. To satirize is not enough. Who today can show a sensible way to relate to modern technology—in art, in medicine, in business, in everyday living—as this new revolution sweeps from America throughout the world?

In the summer of 1977 Dr. Jacob Needleman and I began to plan a series of lectures for Far West Institute in San Francisco, taking as a theme *The Art of Living in the Cultural Revolution*. Two previous lecture series on *Sacred Tradition and Present Need* in 1974 and *On the Way to Self-Knowledge: Sacred Tradition and Psychotherapy* in 1976 had attracted large Sunday evening audiences, though most of the speakers were not well known. When we were offered space for this third series in the Rotunda of the San Francisco Museum of Modern Art we had reason to hope it would also be a useful influence.

The first discussion between Jacob Needleman and Richard Baker-roshi was intended to set the direction for later speakers. For this purpose, it was videotaped. Thus, the conversation between two practiced minds, both trained in the work of self-inquiry, and accustomed to be heard in quiet conditions, took place in a nerve-wracking environment of moving cameras, cables, klieg lights and technicians. Yet the audience, and at times the speakers themselves, saw how the use of the latest technology — if its noise does not distract one from a view of the whole situation — can actually help to produce a sense of the present reality.

But it was not till Paul Caponigro, the photographer of Stonehenge, gave the second talk that it became clear where our theme was leading. Paul had been reluctant to lecture. He said that after pondering the question deeply he had found it was not possible for him to speak on the "art of living" except by turning the question toward his own life and what he had learned in practicing photography. His presentation, he said, including a series of photographs from different periods, would therefore partake of the form of autobiography.

The third lecturer, François Stahly, the sculptor, in an outstanding demonstration of modesty and openness, came at once to the same conclusion, as did several of the later speakers. Winthrop Knowlton actually structured his entire lecture round the story of his own life and business career. When we expressed our thanks to him the next day, he turned the tables by saying how grateful he was for the opportunity for self-examination which our lecture had provided.

Sister Maria José Hobday began by telling us how when she was a young girl her father threw her out of a loving home into the solitude of the desert and about her rare visits to restaurants with her mother, when they would serve her but not her mother, a Seneca Iroquois Indian. But the audience, instead of following these glimpses of her early life, turned to her eagerly for psychological instruction and advice, because that was what they wanted.

They succeeded in bringing out her gifts as a spiritual psychiatrist rather than discovering the unique way she actually is and lives.

Most strivings toward practicing an art of living are thwarted by our limited capacity to perceive all that is going on in our minds at a given moment. In turning to gather up the tangled skeins of one's life, it is difficult to be sincere, to simply look, rather than to innovate or ask the help of others. The lesson has to be learned over and over again that sincerity with oneself is not a virtue to be praised but something that has to be earned and brings its own reward in inner freedom and good judgment. We are grateful to our friends who gave these lectures for putting themselves publicly to this awesome test, with results which will be an inspiration to readers.

John Pentland
San Francisco
December, 1978

Jacob Needleman
and
Richard Baker-Roshi

Jacob Needleman, *Professor of Philosophy at San Francisco State University, is author of* The New Religions *and* A Sense of the Cosmos: The Encounter of Modern Science and Ancient Truth. *Under a grant from the Rockefeller Foundation, he is currently investigating the impact of the new religions on American culture as director of the Program for the Study of New Religions at the Graduate Theological Union in Berkeley.*

Richard Baker-Roshi *received the robe of transmission in 1971 from the late Shunryu Suzuki-Roshi; he is now Abbot of Zen Center in San Francisco, Tassajara, and Green Gulch (all in northern California). For the past seven years he has guided the life of Zen Center in its many aspects: as a monastic training center for American Buddhists, as an urban spiritual community, and as a center of communal farming north of San Francisco.*

NEEDLEMAN: The title of this series of lectures, "The Art of Living in the Cultural Revolution," points in two directions: first, to the fact that we are living in a time of unprecedented change in patterns of living brought about by the intensive application of scientific technology. In every detail of life—how we work, how we eat, how we move around, how we raise children, how we learn, how we die—there is bewildering proliferation of change, extremely rapid external change. So much so that all the patterns of life to which human beings have been accustomed over the centuries are now being turned upside down.

Second, "The Art of Living in the Cultural Revolution" brings the question of how to be human. How to grow, how to be what we are meant to be inwardly, how to live according to conscience in a world where all the external cues and all the external forms are changing? This question, how to live, is certainly an ancient question, but it hasn't always been the main concern in people's lives. Other questions have taken precedence: how to serve God, how to study nature, how to be safe, how to be happy.

But *how to live* points us to the fact that now we have to start from zero; that there's nothing by itself we can turn to out of presupposed trust. It was a question that Plato asked almost two and a half thousand years ago. Socrates asked it in a time when the gods were dying and the physical sciences were no longer in repute. People were torn between the inner world and the outer world. And there was no way of giving oneself completely to either.

Coming to the end of the twentieth century, we're in a similar position. Religion is returning in the form of a new call to inwardness from both Eastern and Western traditions. At the same time, the outer world pulls us with even greater strength in the form of new technologies, innovations that promise us a new world. But people feel they can't give themselves with integrity either to the world promised by the new technologies or to the new religions. So the question of how to live starts from self-inquiry, an inquiry that is neither of the outer world nor of the inner world but rather of the world in-between, the world of myself.

The question of how to live faces us as the question of how to be, how to be toward the ways we have adopted for dealing with nature—the new technologies. What becomes of standards, moral values, not only when they are put against the weaknesses inherent in human nature but against the world of microelectronics, Xerox machines, sophisticated neurochemicals, all the millions of new developments that have already arrived here in our world? Where do we get our values? How to live them? How to incarnate them?—the values to which we are attracted in this world where all the cues, all the names are changing.

What is this technology? What is the inner search in a world that is so powerfully drawing us outward to take a stand for or against these new developments? One could go back to the traditions. . . .

BAKER-ROSHI: Go forward to the traditions. . . .

NEEDLEMAN: Well, one could go forward to the traditions if the traditions were coming forward to us. But if one went back to the traditions as one steps back from oneself, instead of forward as one plunges into a pool—either direction seems to be a problem. Going back, one is told: "Do not get lost in the world of the senses!" But what does that mean now and here? Is that the same world as the world of technology that surrounds us? If the traditions still have the power to help us, we will only discover them by putting our question as completely and intensely as possible, and then we may see who really can help us. In a way, it's a search for people. Can help come from the traditions? Can help come from technology? Can help come from ideas alone? From methods alone? Or from people? What kind of people? What are the real differences between people?

BAKER-ROSHI: It is a search for people, yes, you are right, and a question of what it is to be human! I see almost all change, all conceptual change, as intimate with our hands, with our tools or technologies. Our way of thinking and our relationship to the phenomenal world (transforming or transporting it) is a mutual and interior play, or resonance, each responding, transforming, containing the other's point. Where does that happen?—in the interior that stretches inward in all directions. Yet the problem remains in every society how to meet your self.

3

Where to meet your self? What and where is inward?

What is this new world we are entering into? How do we proceed into it? From where do we proceed? What about the world between thoughts? But we are so *in* conscious, this hardly occurs to us—our existence in the nonconceptual world where direction would be what. What is what? The world of nonthinking—as Dogen Zenji says, "To think nonthinking!"

I agree with you, Zen being a kind of zerotarianism that has to start from zero and, as you say, with conscience, more than consciousness or contact, as control. Perhaps we should start with hedonism, sensation—good or bad—suffer our experience, but let's not start with comfort or the pursuit of happiness.

I think fondly sometimes of Puritan New England; their passionate concern, caring for how the world existed, and for independence, whether the congregations were really independent or not. I don't care for their rejection of those who disagreed with them. Here I prefer the Buddhists, the people of Buddha's time, who similarly had a passionate concern and dialogue with each other about the founding of life, but always with a respect for our common life. Suzuki-Roshi always said not to argue with people, not to try to convince people; that if your life is convincing, that is enough.

These United States were not founded first of all for profit or colonial conquest, but to further the inquiry of what life is. I think it is about time to renew this inquiry in all phases of our life, not as a hobby or idle inquiry but because we really care as a matter of life and death. I think their passionate inquiry was the health of early America. We say to find our state within and without through Great Doubt and Great Faith.

You say not the world of gods and not the outer world, but the in-between world of myself. I like that. In Zen we say the shortcut to meeting yourself is to try to meet others—again without control but contact—to really meet just one other person. Words intended for you alone or just one other person are close to words intended for gods. But start with words intended for one other person. This is where I think every society comes to meeting its tools, finding the direction and use of its tools. Dogen again used to say, "Do not let the sutra, the teachings turn you; you turn the teachings! Meet each other in person!"

Let me tell you a Zen story. I think that is what I should do at this point. There was a fellow named Te Shan—a rather aggressive person, deeply concerned and not entirely in the dark but still caught by the outer world. In this case, the outer world was the Diamond Sutra one of the Wisdom Beyond Wisdom sutras. Not a bad thing to be caught by because it contains the seed of its own destruction. But for Te Shan at this time it was a book of the truth, of what was right, of rules that were already found. He did not understand that the found is lost in advancing civilization or in advancing reality. "The mountain stream rushes so/ The fish cannot stay," are two lines of an old Zen poem.

He had heard about Zen teachers in southern China that he thought heretical because they taught that transmission is outside the scriptures and that there should be no dependence on the word. So he decided to visit southern China and straighten them out with his great learning of the Diamond Sutra.

Books were rather large in those days, and the sutra and commentaries became a great box that he carried on his back. Finally reaching the southern part of China, he stopped to rest. He entered a small tea shop along the road and asked for a cup of tea and a kind of fried cake, the characters for which mean something like to lighten up your mind, or to refresh yourself.

The woman of the shop was very sharp and spotted him right away as an alert if benighted fellow. She asked what the box was he was carrying. He said, "The Diamond Sutra. I am a master of the Diamond Sutra." She was master of herself and said, "Does not the Diamond Sutra say 'past mind is ungraspable, present mind is ungraspable, and future mind is ungraspable'? With what mind will you take this cake?" (What mind will you refresh?) Te Shan was stopped and smart enough to know when he did not know.

One of Nagarjuna's four propositions is to know when you do not know, or rather to try hard enough to actually know when you have exhausted a possibility and then to have the reality and rigor to act on that realization. This is more than most of us know. In fact, most of us never care about anything enough to exhaust or reach its possibilities. We lack the courage and energy to try fully enough to chance failing, to actually fail. Dogen calls this real life, one continuous mistake.

So Te Shan was stopped and knew it; but still a male chauvinist, he asked, "Are there any good teachers around here?" Kindly she directed him to Lung T'an, a famous teacher who lived a few miles away. The Chinese characters for Lung T'an mean dragon lake or abyss. So when Te Shan reached Lung T'an's temple and he was given admittance, he, in a rather Zennie way and pressing the idea of emptiness (of zero), said, "I have come here, yet I see neither dragon nor lake." Lung T'an just then stepped out from behind a screen and said, "You are meeting Lung T'an in person."

Te Shan was stopped again, and he bowed and withdrew. Later in the evening he returned to Lung T'an's room and just stood in attendance until late at night. Finally Lung T'an said, "Why don't you go?" Te Shan went out onto the veranda and turned and said, "It has become pitch dark." Lung T'an handed him a lantern and, as Te Shan stepped outside with it, Lung T'an leaned and blew it out. Suddenly Te Shan was enlightened. He entered that space which is neither light nor dark, where actual teaching occurs, where we meet each other and meet ourself. He immediately and deeply bowed to Lung T'an, who said, "What have you seen that you bow?" Te Shan said, "I will never again doubt that the teaching is outside the scriptures."

This is to be completely exposed, your guts in your ears, eyes, and mouth. In person!

One reason I told this story is that I want to give us some vocabulary for this discussion of what the art of living is about. Jerry Needleman himself, in one of his books, has used the phrase *passive attention,* which I find very useful. I'll probably get it mixed up, but I would like to share it now as a Buddhist term. He uses the example of a magician with a pitcher that looks like an ordinary pitcher of milk, but actually the white liquid is in an inner lining. So actually nothing's being poured. But because of your passive attention, you assume it is a pitcher of milk. Most of our mental activity is rough and passive because of a similar lack of attention. It is lined with assumptions. The first of the Four Noble Truths of Buddhism is that there is suffering, and the second is that there is a cause of suffering. And the cause of suffering resides in our mental and physical actions, which are usually lost or hidden in our passive attention, in our inconsciousness. So how do we make our mental and physical actions accessible? How to break through passive attention? How, like Lung T'an, do you meet someone in person? Am I meeting you all in person?

Western philosophy distinguishes the material world from the mental world. But in the nineteenth century, when Friedrich Wöhler synthesized urea, that distinction was blurred, and the people of that time chose to move toward seeing everything as material. If urea can be synthesized from completely inert, non-sentient material, when before this urea was thought to be only made by organic beings, then people began to think we are just combinations of inert stuff that even can be genetically manufactured or engineered. But that arrow points both ways; maybe we should consider everything to be organic, changing in a way that is little different from consciousness. In Zen we are not much concerned with the distinction between material and mind. We are much more interested in conditioned mind and unconditioned mind—unconditioned mind which is identified with everything all at once, including the phenomenal world.

Let me tell another story. Chao Chou, who did not shout or beat with the stick, was said to have lips which breathed light and fire. Once Chao Chou, when he was a student, asked Nan Ch'uan, "What is the Way?" Nan Ch'uan answered, "Ordinary mind (or everyday mind) is the Way." Now you must stop and think a minute. What is this ordinary mind? Really ordinary? Special? Or does Nan Ch'uan mean the usual mind not involved in being special? So you can understand Chao Chou's question, "This ordinary mind, how do I approach it?" Ch'uan said, "If you turn toward it, you turn away from it." Then you can understand Chao's next question, "How do I know when no attempt is the Way?" Nan Ch'uan answered, "The Way is not in the realm of knowing or not knowing. Knowing is an illusion, and not knowing is blankness. True arrival is vastness, no-doubt. What is there to affirm or deny?" In another context Dogen said, "Arrival hinders arrival."

So tonight we can ask what is this ordinary mind formed by and connected to the world through television, radios, newspapers, magazines, books, computers, endless interpretations? Can we trust this ordinary mind, or do we want to turn away from it not toward it? Is there some essential ordinary mind? Where, how, can we find guidance? Synthesized intelligence? Humans bred in test tubes for what characteristics and implanted in ordinary wombs? Does the essential formative relationship with the mother end at birth? Is the rest sociology? Can we separate biology and sociology? A millionaire clones himself or wants to. Why, in anyone's name?

NEEDLEMAN: I think the vocabulary you have given is enough; anything that brings us to this point of attention would be more than enough. It does resonate in us. But the question is: How deep does it go? And how do you take into account that, even though it's on television and in the air, practically the truth we need may not enter very deeply precisely because we have agreed to it so quickly. How are we going to live the truth about attention rather than dream it? Does the modern situation make us say *yes* to new ideas so quickly that we never see the *no* that is going to be there when we really try to live them?

BAKER-ROSHI: Exactly. Gregory Bateson points out how difficult it is to teach graduate students today because for them everything is relative, they agree with whatever you say. You present them with something, and they don't know that they don't know. You say something, and they say, "Oh yeah, yeah," and they haven't heard at all.

I was party to a conversation the other day in which one person said, "Well, Coyote didn't really create the world, even in Indian culture they took it with a grain of salt that Coyote created the world." And this other person said, "You know I completely believed in Adam and Eve, and the blood—that the wine was the blood of Christ and the wafer, the bread was the body of Christ. I completely believed all that. And then I found out that it didn't work, and it changed me." Remarkable that you can only really try on something by believing in it, or at least trying to believe in it, and that you really find out that something doesn't work by first believing in it. In Zen we call this the work of Great Doubt and Great Faith. It is the way you locate yourself existentially— to try your life thoroughly and find out what doesn't work, then you really know. This is Gregory's idea, that you can't teach most American students, even graduate students, because they don't say, "Oh my God, that completely revolutionizes my thinking;" they just agree with everything.

NEEDLEMAN: No, I'm not speaking about that, exactly. It's not so much the graduate student in all of us. Certainly, if it were possible, as Kierkegaard said, to believe passionately in something, then even if it's an error it will lead you to the truth. But the whole point is we don't have the wholeness even to do that. If we had, we'd already be different than we are. Everybody wants to begin higher than where we are, with commitment. But where does that commitment become merely a form of fantasy, and where is it a reality; what is real commitment to an idea or an experiment? Things are arranged so comfortably for us because of our technology, our science, that the first question to be faced is, where do I really pay for what I believe in; how do I start?

BAKER-ROSHI: One thing I have found out trying to wend through our materialistic and scientific culture is that it is advisable to turn toward the difficulties in your life and to never remove yourself from danger. When you are always trying to make your life comfortable, not out on a limb, you soon are in trouble. How do you get to the point where there's commitment? You know, you just get committed, you decide to do it, there's no dial under your arm that you can turn toward commitment. It is not done by awakening some spiritual powers; you just decide. You have to act in the realm of what's available to you. You have to put yourself out on a limb. And in Zen we experiment with this all the time. You follow through even on your mistakes. A simple example is, from memory you start dialing somebody, say in New York or someplace, then halfway through dialing you suspect it is a wrong number. If you're practicing Zen, you continue. Let the person answer, pick it up on the other end. You may say, "Oh, I thought it might be the wrong number, I'm sorry, how are things in Florida?" And then you take the bill and pay it. If you know you are going to follow through, if you're always going to take the consequences for what you do, you become much more alert. So responsibility has a lot to do with it.

NEEDLEMAN: I see we're coming back to this question of my attention, my alertness, my inner state. We have forms of living —education, family, children, vocation, laws. Where do you find a bridge that takes us back into everyday life from that very extraordinary thing you're speaking about—this "dialing of the telephone" and that rare moment of seeing and accepting that one's attention has gone, whether it's through letting the phone company bill you for it or letting the inner phone company bill you for it, but accepting that moment when one is aware of the inner state. Because then one "hangs up the phone" and goes out into life, or what we call life. In meditation perhaps it is possible to touch this understanding of myself, of the forces of consciousness. But I can't always be in meditation. I can't always be sitting. Now what is it, that bridge that connects us, for example, to our relationships with others? And aren't you speaking about something which also means an awakening of a sort of faculty within us that can know the value of things? We're speaking about values, obviously, not speaking just about making mistakes in life.

BAKER-ROSHI: But as Dogen-Zenji says, life is one continuous mistake, and we are being billed for them all the time. *Upaya,* skillful means, also means that the world is not repeatable, and yet right now I am being transmitted into repetition through the television camera.

NEEDLEMAN: Though not yet cloned.

BAKER-ROSHI: Not yet cloned. You know, I don't usually let my lectures within Zen Center be taped. Sometimes we do, but I am more interested in hearing from whoever is listening. You are the recorder, and if you miss it, all right—but it's wonderful hearing from you.

QUESTION: What is the validity of our living? Are we very much oriented toward technology because we tend to think that ultimately scientific verification is the most valid?

NEEDLEMAN: I agree that our thinking is conditioned by scientific forms, and one of the problems of the spiritual traditions is how to take that into account in transmitting their teaching. We had a lecture series several years ago about the traditions, where this became a very focused question—whether the traditional forms of teaching, the myth, symbols, were geared at all to a mind so conditioned as ours is by scientific thinking. How to transmit these teachings to such a mind as ours without their being dictated to by scientific forms? How to use these forms as a kind of *upaya,* if you like, and yet penetrate beneath them. I think this is one of the biggest questions that the traditions are facing.

BAKER-ROSHI: A main problem a person practicing meditation faces today in relationship to so-called scientific truths and from the influence of science is that we are always trying to get some outside confirmation of our experience and trying to make sure something is true (or safe) before we do it.

Here is a brief story. A friend of mine brought his crazy brother, who is flipping out, to New York in a car. The boy, young man, realized that he couldn't hold a job, and my friend was talking with him about psychiatrists. He was agreeable as they were leaving California, but, at the same time, he was trying to draw his so-called sane brother into his so-called crazy world. By the time they reached Ohio, he had. This friend, the sane one, was beginning to feel very bizarre; he began to see the world from his crazy brother's point of view. Actually, we are always doing that, we are trying to bring each other into our own world, sane or crazy.

We have an interior dialogue in which we are talking to ourselves all the time, trying to adjust things, and we don't really let lust, anger, hatred, delusion, confusion, and all the things we have done (which if we really looked at we would feel miserable about) come up. Our interior dialogue keeps making adjustments, and, further, we make everybody else participate in the exterior version of this dialogue, like actors in our own theater.

So if you are practicing, one of the first things is to profoundly let everyone alone, to try at least not to be always drawing people into your world, but at the same time without denying or hiding your own world. This is also transmission outside the scriptures, and transmission outside the media, television, newspapers, books, and words, too. In Zen we are concentrated on immediacy (no media); immediacy means without hesitation, without an outside observer, trusting yourself because you have no alternative. As you can see from your own dreams and your daily life, mostly our interior and exterior definitions don't correspond very well. It is the work and power of meditation to bring these two together and to move more into the realm of the immediate.

NEEDLEMAN: Well, how would someone then come to want to meditate if it hasn't been first communicated through the media, as it were? It would be just a compassionate reaching out?

BAKER-ROSHI: The traditional way is through in-person contact. Somebody's brother or sister or friend shows up. So far our experience has been that people who come through the equivalent of *Time* magazine do not know what they are getting into and have no acceptance or understanding of process. History moves at such a pace for them that there are no actions, just events.

NEEDLEMAN: Well, I don't mean *Time* magazine, but I mean how to communicate help to the beginner—not the beginner's mind but the beginner? If you saw somebody who wants to be immediate, it's already not immediate.

BAKER-ROSHI: That's right. Beginner's mind is the same in the beginner and the expert.

NEEDLEMAN: I think we are all sort of beginners over and over again.

QUESTION: What do I do beyond being real or truthful to my immediate life?

BAKER-ROSHI: As a child you grow up involved with finding *your* identity, but at some point you shift to recognizing *our* identity. This wider identity, in a Buddhist metaphor, is the great ocean merging into a single drop (not the drop merging into the great ocean). Or again, how does a particle act in terms of a whole field, how does it receive so rapidly all the information about what's going on throughout the field? As someone said, How does everywhere get here?

NEEDLEMAN: There's another side of it perhaps. Apart from this search to become real, what do you do in life? All these things that people do, they have jobs, families, careers; they are artists. People want these forms, but they don't know why, they don't know what they're for. What is a family for? What is education for? Is this the question you're asking? I think that is the question.

QUESTION: There's one part of me receives the answer you've just given, which I feared . . . it's enough to be real . . . it's ample.

BAKER-ROSHI: If you do that, it communicates everywhere.

NEEDLEMAN: By living a life of interior search, one believes that all by itself it will communicate to the whole of your life. But I don't think you're speaking about the external versus the internal, but of the different parts of ourselves. The part of myself that's involved with an inner search or an interiority or a meditation—and the part of oneself that is activated when one goes through one's daily life, day by day. How can one simply believe that one of these parts will all by itself transmit to the other parts, other than in a superficial transitory way?

BAKER-ROSHI: If a crazy person walks into a room, it usually makes everybody nervous. If somebody who is coherent walks into a room, it has the opposite effect. Noticing this, the emphasis in Buddhist tradition is to aim at creating optimal individuals, optimal communities, with the confidence that this is the most effective and real way to reach individuals and the whole society.

You know, in the meditation hall we return the bow of the person standing on the left and the right and the person standing facing us across the room. If I bow to my seat before sitting down, then the people on my left and right bow, and the person across the way bows, and according to the rule it stops there. But if there were no rule and everyone returned each other's bows, to the left and right, rippling down the aisles and across the way, it would spread almost instantaneously throughout the room, and you would quickly have a mass of bowing people tangled up in the middle of the room. But even though we stop the physical bow with the rule, the bow still passes throughout the room, throughout the world.

A good joke will pass very rapidly, very rapidly by word of mouth across the country. A bad joke needs television. So I think it is not necessary, it is better not to make distinctions between public and private, big responsibilities and small responsibilities. So the effort is to be every occasion you have or are. What other choice do you have? You are sitting right there—not trapped. Please go—through being here.

QUESTION: What is the responsibility in a world where, for instance, if you buy tuna, you are responsible in some way for the slaughter of dolphins, if you buy foreign goods, you are responsible for the monetary imbalance worldwide and the loss of American jobs, etc., and you can also consider the foreign jobs in two seconds? Would it be possible for us to agree on a simple consensus that would establish the limits of responsibility that would let us live without guilt?

BAKER-ROSHI: It is necessary that we let the bow stop somewhere, so we can act, but still knowing our responsibility; knowing and being able to bear that creation and destruction are a single pulse.

NEEDLEMAN: Isn't it part of self-inquiry to see where one's moral standards have come from, what one's emotions such as guilt are made of? To question the sense of guilt itself or the moral opinions that have come to one from God knows where and have been taken in in this passive form that we've been speaking about? Perhaps it's not that the standards need to be scrutinized but the way they've been taken in and reacted to. Is there a part of oneself that is free from "morality" in order to be really moral? Believing in every subjective reaction is a particularly intriguing problem today when we are so pummeled with statements, thoughts, information, moral verities coming from all sorts of places, and our emotions themselves may not really be ours in any fundamental sense.

Maybe one has to get back to this problem of a bridge between the inner world and outer life. If you have a kind of undaunted attention to yourself without taking sides one way or the other, how come that gets lost immediately when the outer problems come in? I think one has to face the question of what we mean by responsibility. Is it just something that we're told would happen? What is a free human being? Is it somebody who has something which is bigger than the parts that are always reacting? Does courage ever come from anything but contact with the real feeling, a total feeling about it? What helps us to contact our real feeling about anything? How much of what we suffer from, our guilt and so forth, is real? And do we have any real feelings— which is what I take to be the meaning of conscience?

BAKER-ROSHI: I find the main thing is to find out how to trust yourself, so that you know what you want to do and know that what comes up in you, you can trust. Mountains, trees, and dogs do not doubt themselves; why do we? Nan Ch'uan said the Way is no-doubt.

During a time when some Japanese carpenters were working on a building in this country, I was watching the master carpenter placing rocks. A line of Americans were passing him the rocks, and he would take and use immediately whatever rock was handed him. So the decision-making passed very rapidly down the line to the first person picking up the rock, because he knew that whatever rock he picked up would go without further reflection directly into the wall. We have to work directly with ourselves in an experimental way until we get to what is our heart's content. It is a real effort and not easy.

Usually if you make a big decision, you'll say, "That was just something I had to do, I had no choice." The decision makes you. But how to get in touch with that? You usually know what you want to do, really, but don't like doing it.

I would like to change the subject and tell you a short story that illustrates for me the authority we give to a person with a tool, weapon, or machine. One day at the University of California, when I was a graduate student, I was waiting in a long line of maybe twenty-five or thirty-five people. All of us were waiting at this one small window to make some change in our schedules. There were quite a few windows, but only one was open. In the room behind the windows I could hear many people talking, joking, phones ringing, and so forth. I was suddenly reminded that people don't know how to deal with machinery, with phones, except by answering them, while they will keep many live bodies standing in long lines. So I walked across the lobby, in sight of the entire line, into a phone booth and dialed the number of the university and was transferred into the room behind the windows, where the phone was answered. I said, "Could I change such and such a course," and they said, "Fine." I said, "Thank you," and hung up. Then I debated for a while the logistics, politics, and futility of having every other person line up at the phone booth or jam the lines with requests that they open more windows. Here are actual human beings with all their molecules, atomic and human energy, waiting—and the phone is responded to, not the people.

Another problem brought to us by technology is that, with the physical and electronic transportation available, people can arrive at your doorstep in such numbers, and in so many forms—letters, telephone, television, newspapers, and so forth—that there is no way to cope with it all. A rule I've made for myself is that, if a person is there in person, I respond to them above everything else. But I do enjoy the phone. You have somebody talking right in your ear, pauses, breath, and you are in their ear; but still it's not the same as in person. I don't know how to solve this one, for example, even what to do with the video and written transcription that this discussion will turn into. A person does not come and visit you early in the morning or late in the evening, but people will phone at all hours of the day and night. I am always seeking ways to manage just the phone and letters; so far television, film, and tapes are beyond me.

QUESTION: Are your mistakes important to your experience of life?

BAKER-ROSHI: Mistakes and corrections. If you are at a party and it crosses your mind, "Maybe I should leave," you get up and leave. You can trust that thought instead of saying, "Well, I'll stay for a little longer." It is a way of experimenting with yourself.

NEEDLEMAN: I think you're talking about having an inner aim while you have outer life. What is this fear or attraction that causes people to either promote technology as the new world, as the answer to all human problems; or to be so afraid of it, that it's destroying some mystery in human life. It is also a question of evaluating technology itself. How much of myself do I give to these things—how much of my inner force—and how much do I keep for myself? It's the question of the telephone, only on a bigger scale.

BAKER-ROSHI: If the machine, or media, or whatever reduces "in person," reduces danger, reduces responsibility—if it does this or makes things secondhand or thirdhand, I tend to shy away from it. Perhaps for moral and philosophical reasons, but mostly because it is just not interesting, the level of intensity is not satisfying. I become bored.

Let me tell a story about Rusty Schweikert. Rusty was the first person to go out on the end of one of those umbilical cords and float around in space. For a long time he asked himself repeatedly, "What is it going to be like in outer space—to have an almost heavenly view of earth?" Actually about half the astronauts, from what I'm told, had quite remarkable experiences, and half just came back like they had driven their Fords down the street or taken an ordinary flight. Anyway, Rusty wondered what the great thoughts of mankind are going to be like when you see the whole earth in outer space. So he stuck in his boot a list of what, I don't know who, but perhaps what Shakespeare, Spinoza, Socrates, and Christ had said. But you get up there, and of course they have you programmed, every minute is programmed, and you are always behind schedule. You don't have the time to think about anything. But while he was out floating free of the spacecraft, his friend was taking his picture according to schedule when the camera jammed. So for five minutes Rusty had nothing to do. He was floating in space and free from his schedule. He started to reach for his boot where he had tucked away a few of the great thoughts of humanity, but he thought he would just look, and he turned and looked at the earth—and he was wiped out, the earth indescribably floating there.

Rusty says that the astronauts who had this kind of experience prepared for it. They thought about it beforehand, they did something like get these short quotations in their boot. Their experience was characterized by being ready and, at the same time, by being taken unaware. They had some readiness in them, even in the midst of all the machinery.

NEEDLEMAN: The openess that another astronaut, Ed Mitchell, had when he described the earth and saw all the wars and realized what an absurd tragedy it is, because the earth is really one. Down there everybody is setting themselves off against other people, but he could feel its oneness from his point of view. But when he got back, he couldn't keep that feeling. Isn't this what we need to watch just as carefully as possible? Somehow, at least the way I approach it, you have to find out how to keep that feeling, that vast feeling or wider mind at the same time as you're dealing with the specificity of things.

BAKER-ROSHI: I would like to say one last thing. I was asked to take Gregory Bateson's place in this discussion, because he could not be here. I hope in some way I have been able to express ideas that are consonant with his own and that reflect at least a measure of what I have learned from his presence, conversation, and books. He is a very great man, who stands just a little bit ahead of what anyone is yet able to recognize as the direction we are almost certainly headed. His observations and wisdom are essential.

Paul Caponigro

Paul Caponigro has long been recognized as one of the great contemporary American photographers. A resident of New Mexico, he has just completed a portfolio of extraordinary pictures of Stonehenge and the megaliths of Britain. Other examples of his work may be found in the collections of numerous museums throughout the United States.

I HAVE LEARNED that photography has a lot to teach me if I can remain open to it and stay close to the idea of developing it as a craft. I was greatly privileged, through the aid of a Guggenheim Fellowship around 1966, to put the craft I had developed in photography at the service of stones. The stones affected me deeply about that time. I will begin with my early work, and we'll move along toward that time and that place when I met the stones. I will try to express as best I can how they taught me, how I used my medium to try and bring some of what I was receiving back to you.

Nature was one of my first teachers. I decided at a certain point that I would photograph nature to try and learn as much as possible. Benny Chin was very encouraging in that sense. He simply said there's nothing to do except get to work, handed me his camera, tripod, instructed me in the use of materials, and said, "Now go and work."

I learned and felt something about the forces of nature. I tried to record it, as best I could, on film and to make the best prints I could, to share what I saw and felt about nature. At times she was quite delicate. I was interested in the quiet moods that she would present—the rhythms, the very gentle surface activity of Mother Nature. She presented me with some forms—snow on branches. There was a world of material with which to work, to make pictures, and again to feel the forces that would create these forms, shapes, and surfaces. Around 1965 I began to photograph the sunflower. Could it be photographed to look like the sun? I also wanted to know if the sunflower could look like a star. My imagination wanted to travel a bit, I wanted to go further than just working with surfaces. I saw a tree in a leaf. I was probing for some larger principles, and I even managed to get a galaxy in an apple. I worked quite a while with nature—details, close-ups, larger landscapes, feeling my way through whatever nature would offer—her forces, surfaces.

Then something started prompting me to look at surfaces in a different way. I'd been photographing forms, surface textures, light. But one particular photograph did something to the space that was not logical. One can look at it and say, oh yes, a stand of trees, a river. But there's something about the space in this photograph that throws you for a slight loop. You can figure it out, your mind will stop and think about it. But on the first encounter, space within the photo has been changed. And this was important to me at that time, because I wanted to get beyond surfaces. I wanted to find a way to understand why I was reacting to forces which were present, although not really seen by the eye. So this early part of my photographic career was the involvement with the tactile sensations, with the light, with everything solid that you would come in contact with and know physically. But there was a new direction for me, regarding my work and my own questions about myself: How can I start photographing what's behind the object? There was an important photo also in the sunflower series [a close-up of the flower's center], because those

Cabbage leaf.
1965.

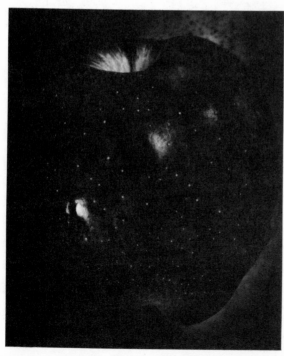

Apple.
1964.

Kilclooney dolmen.
Donegal, Ireland.

Redding Woods, Connecticut.
1968.

Proleek dolmen.
Ireland.

Kiltiernan dolmen.
County Dublin.

Lough Crew cairns.
County Meath, Ireland.

Stone and Tree.
Avebury, England, 1967.

Stonehenge.
1970.

Kermario alignments.
Carnac, Brittany, France, 1967.

New Grange.
1967.

Stonehenge.
1972.

Stonehenge.

many interlocking spirals reminded me of the forces that were at work on a tremendous scale in the universe as well as the smaller forces reflected in the lower levels.

In 1966 I was awarded a Guggenheim Fellowship. During the late 1950s and into the early 1960s I had become interested in ancient art. I was visiting museums, looking at books, questioning what ancient man revealed, what was present in his art that was affecting me so. It was nothing I can describe easily. I was simply pulled to it. Originally I had intended to go to Egypt and photograph the great temples there, some of the sculptures, some of the reliefs. I wanted, in the same way I had learned from photography and nature, to learn from ancient man by photographing what he had produced. At that time it was politically difficult to go to Egypt; that is, the Americans were not on very good terms with Egyptians. So instead I decided to go to Ireland, where I could study the Celtic culture—those high crosses, those early stone huts the monks used, and whatever I could find that belonged to ancient man. I wanted to be exposed to him in order to learn.

As I worked at photographing the crosses and churches, I encountered this group of stones. The configuration is known as a *dolmen,* which, literally translated from the Breton language, means stone table. I had no idea if the man who owned the land had put them there or how they had gotten there, but the effect on me was as if a child had seen a bison for the very first time, had just encountered it in the field. I was greatly awed. I didn't really understand why, but I was mystified and drawn to those stones. It was as if a meteorite had dropped out of the sky—that's how that first dolmen hit me. I began to investigate. I changed my project on recording Celtic art—the high crosses, the early churches—and I simply went about in the field with maps, aided by archeologist friends who indicated the historic period of the stones and where to find them. I simply had to be in the presence of these stones and continue to work with and experience them.

I did discover that there were groups of stones as well as single standing stones. But there weren't many people who could explain them to me. Were they left in the wake of that great glacial period? Did man put them there? If so, how did he get them there? These are quite massive pieces of stone. There was an irresistible something about the stones, and I'm sorry, I can only call it a force. However these particular stones got there, they had an atmosphere, and I began to realize that it was the atmosphere that was around these stones that was drawing me in. It took me maybe three or four months of real consternation and concern. I was responsible to Guggenheim; what was I doing? Well, I finally decided that I would do it.

The stones did have a language. They even spoke things at me, those markings on the stones. They had a way of pulling you toward them, and they could also speak. The ten-year involvement was my attempt at understanding the language of the stones. They came up out of the earth and assumed an attitude which I gradually began to realize was that of ancient man and something belonging to his aspiration. I began to feel that ancient man was symbolically raising some of the most solid parts of earth (and you could apply that idea to the individual physical body), that he was taking the most difficult parts, the solid parts of earth, and raising them up. The feats of balance are quite astonishing. They've been there for two thousand years, four thousand years, it's disputed among the archeologists. Possibly they go as far back as six thousand years B.C. The nobility in these stones so struck me that I decided to give up everything else, including my photography, in order to communicate with them. I was getting criticism from my fellow photographers at that time—"Whatever happened to those beautiful nature landscapes you were making, and those lovely details?" they would say. "Why are you doing this kind of photography when your art is at stake?" Well, it just didn't matter, because I simply had to know what ancient man was saying through the stones.

Another type of stone configuration is the stone circle. Ancient man was often making stone circles on the earth. Incidentally, my photographs were all taken through the British Isles and down into France and much of Western Europe. This is where most of the different types of stone monuments are found. And the Irish have a particular feeling about these ancient stones; they won't disturb them. They will clear land endlessly in order to use it for grazing and planting, and they'll remove the trees, but if a tree is too close to a stone circle, they'll not touch the tree. It shows their reverence—they sense that there is something special about these places that is not to be disturbed.

The circle was very important to ancient man. It seemed to be a sacred space for him. Much earlier, the spaces man created were of earth. Later he created the stone circles, which functioned for another purpose. How very simple but how absolutely effective his expression of setting apart a piece of the earth for a special purpose. The double circle interested me because I found that it was appearing in different ways. They etched it into their stones. It's a language on that stone that the archeologist has yet to decipher. One of the great circles in England is known as the Avebury Stone Circle. It's about twenty miles north of Stonehenge and much older. Again, that double circle seemed to be repeating itself at Avebury. I haven't got hold of what that double circle means. They began with the earth. They piled the earth and made their circles, and within and without that they would place their stones.

Then I came to what are known as *cairns*—the erection of stone chambers and, again, the piling of earth over the chambers, surrounding it with stones to keep the earth from slipping away. One of the largest cairns in Ireland is known as Maeve's Cairn. Maeve, in Irish mythology, was a rather difficult queen. When she died, she was interred under this cairn, according to myth, and every year the Irish, still to this day, will carry stones along the pathway from the bottom of the mountain up the hill and place them on the cairn to be certain she doesn't get out. They're keeping those forces within. Very often you'll find these cairns on high places, giving an uplifting experience, a feeling of the vastness of the space around, and thereby also helping the religious feeling.

Archeology hasn't really determined yet what the function of these cairns were. It's easy enough to say they were burial mounds for their kings, but I spent six years visiting these places, and my feelings included more than that. It could well have been that some served as places to inter their great men, but in going inside several cairns, in moving around them, there was quite another sense that I felt, which was that men would enter the earth—they would reenter the womb of Mother Earth—for another purpose. If to die, they will leave their bones there, but I also felt that they released their spirit in there and could get to other dimensions. So they would enter the earth, they would enter symbolically their own bodies for the purpose of discovering what all those forces are about: What really do we have inside? Who are we? if you like. This was a way, in my opinion, of isolating themselves, of placing themselves in an area where they would not be subject to so many outer forces. They had a chance to inwardly concentrate. So I feel they were ritual and meditation places as well as burial places.

Cairn translated, by the way, means stone mound. When you go inside a cairn, you find small chambers, with inscriptions on the stones. What the inscriptions are telling man, I don't know. Perhaps instructions for passing to the other world. They may well be messages about what to look for within yourself, within that chamber, to touch other dimensions. The very strong sense that I got from these cairns was that they seemed to go right into Mother Earth. And to me it was as if they were entering the earth to find out about a mystery. These standing stones, to me, seem to speak about the resurrection, an upliftment. There is this inward action in the cairn and tumulus and then there is an upward thrust in the standing stones, which eventually seemed a simultaneous action inward in the cairn and upward in the dolmen and standing stone.

A *tumulus* is constructed on basically the same principle as a cairn. They also have an avenue of stones and entrance. In the center you find chambers, either for burial or for meditation, and they cover the whole thing with earth. There is an entrance, a passage, and then some chambers off to the side and in the center. They look like hills from a distance, but if you look closer you may find the entrance, you may even sometimes get into some of them; not all of them are accessible. New Grange is a very famous tumulus in Europe. Archeologists are always visiting there and looking for new information. I think it has a very strong impact on the individual. I can remember my first visit. The spiral markings on the stones reminded me very much of the forces that are unseen, that work on so many levels. Once past those spirals, you make your entrance into the chamber. You must, incidentally, bend down to get into that entrance, which is, in a sense, a humbling. You then continue up the passage, and very gradually the ceiling of stones is lifting until you finally get to the central chamber, where you can stand upright. On my first encounter it was as if I had seen Chartres cathedral for the first time. They're made of rude stones by men that are called barbarians by some archeologists and historians, but the sophistication of these designs, the sense of placement of the stones, was an awesome experience for me. I was silenced. These were not just places to bury a king. This was a place that one came to worship, to be silent, a chance to go inward.

There are three very important tumuli in County Meath, Ireland, all within a radius of three-quarters of a mile—Dowth, New Grange, and Knowth. You can see in the photographs how carefully the mounds were built up by man—layers of earth, clay, and stone, successively—and then surrounded by very large stones to keep that whole complex from slipping away in time. I think those outer inscribed stones are as if saying something to protect the inner contents. My feeling was that the inscriptions on these stones were speaking about forces—forces in life, forces perhaps that ancient man was much more in touch with, perhaps understood a lot better than we do today.

I'd like to give you a very personal experience. This particular trinity of tumuli, after I worked with them for maybe two or three years, began to impart each a very distinct sensation, a specific quality. That first one, known as Dowth, I only wanted to enter once, because it literally frightened me. I felt that it was a place where purgation could take place. You had to go in, face it, do something within yourself in that place for the sake of purging and overcoming the fear. The second tumulus was a place of experiencing what in man we might call the religious. I was literally awed and silenced when inside New Grange. In and around the third tumulus, Knowth, there was absolute joy; the place emanated pure joy. That trilogy seemed very significant and was possibly one of my first teachings from those ancient places. It wasn't always easy to get a sense of expressing the circle in my pictures, but I was always very happy to be with these stones; they always gave off a feeling good to be near, a bit ominous at times, and yet it belonged to the circle.

Down in Brittany, at Carnac, there are what are known as the Kermario alignments. This alignment of stones stands tall at one end of the line and gradually tapers down as they move over a three-quarter mile distance, to about two feet. The purpose I don't really know, and the stones wouldn't tell me—not right away. When I did ask these stones, I began to learn the language of stone, which was: silence. I had to learn silence. I had already decided that I was going to turn my craft over to recording these stones and share the results with others. But it took me quite a while to realize that, to get any answers (for myself, of course), I had to learn silence. That was the language of stone. In that silence these stones told me that they were sentinels to eternity.

In the Outer Hebrides, on the Isle of Lewis in the north of Scotland, is another rather wonderful circle that had quite an impact on me, Callanish. Those stones felt as if they had walked there during some time period which I really cannot fathom—I think maybe no-time. They seemed to have assembled for a very important conference and to have some very important things to say to one another. What I'm really saying is that one of these stones is a self-portrait, and it's addressing a very important personage that exists as the central stone. Depending on the way in which the question is put, how it's felt, such and such an answer would be given by the center stone. That stone is a high priest. Another stone is pointing to the sun.

Finally, we come to the famous Stonehenge monument, one of the great circles of the British Isles. Archeology says that it took possibly four thousand years to complete, and that about three or four thousand B.C. they began construction with that earth circle on the outside. Within that they placed some small stones, and maybe two thousand years later those large uprights in the center were finally placed. I'm sure most people have read that there are a lot of ideas about what purpose Stonehenge served—that it was an astronomical clock and observatory. I'm sure it did function as such; but again, my experience, my personal reaction, was of the atmosphere of the place and what that can bring you to. I was fortunate to have a great deal of time alone there to contact the site.

One of the mistakes in my photography was an unintentional double exposure. There is a lot of work being done these days with multiple images overlaying and the likes of that, but I've never done that kind of work; I'm pretty much a straight photographer. I was very pleased with this particular double exposure accident, because it gives a sense of a time past—many years, thousands of years, I don't know, but it simply gave the feeling

that Stonehenge was eternal. That double exposure overlaid that
idea with the presence of those stones you can experience today.

This double exposure is the first print of the portfolio which I
have recently completed. I decided to try to digest what I had
gotten from the photographing of Stonehenge; and, after taking
maybe four hundred or five hundred negatives, I have printed
twelve negatives in an edition of sixty sets, which I'm presenting
as a portfolio. Here is a quotation from the introduction which
I have written for the portfolio:

> Stonehenge is a great achievement of Neolithic man. It stands on a
> plain in England where there is a 360 degree view of the horizon.
> This configuration of stones, with its massive uprights and lintels, has
> remained an enigma for centuries. Construction of this impressive and
> sophisticated monument is thought to have begun around 2,500 B.C.,
> with the formation of an earthen mound, 320 feet in diameter. The
> astonishing inner trilithons in the outer ring of stones were probably
> completed around 1,500 B.C. However, recent methods of tree-ring
> dating hinted further mystery. Stonehenge could easily be a thousand
> years older. Many believe that this ancient circle functioned as an
> observatory for the study of the heavenly luminaries, and served a
> priesthood in arranging an annual calendar of religious ceremonies
> and festivals. With others, attention is focused on the sheer physical
> accomplishment. But for those who dwell and ponder deeper into this
> magical arrangement, there's more. An indefinable force persists and
> pervades. The effect is to silence one with wonder. These uncompro-
> mising stones radiate an awesome prescience. Although the uprights
> and lintels obviously served as windows and doors, one senses a
> greatness coming through yet another door; a greatness which per-
> severes in another dimension, and causes chronological time to melt
> away. There is indeed mystery here, of boundaries that unbind, and
> of instruments for the measuring of time which leads to the timeless.
> We may never know for certain why ancient man assembled these
> stones, but man's humanity can sense that nobility and feel the aspira-
> tion that materialized into a great internal idea. Sentinel-like, these
> stones stand as if encompassing all inner and outer boundaries. Stones
> uplifted, aspiring and balanced. Stones chanting a ring of protective
> power for the sacred space within.

To finish with, a word about my most favorite ancient stone
complex: the dolmen, a configuration of very massive, upright
stones. On top is placed a great crushing weight, known as the

capstone. The lifting of the stone is such an aspirational act. They are lifted, massive weights, rendering them weightless. It's a wonderful internal idea, and incredibly demonstrated by ancient man through the real weight of stone. If you are there, you can touch the stone; you know it's heavy, you sense its weight. In fact, you very often don't want to go too close, wondering whether they might collapse. They've been standing there for some three to four thousand years, but they float; they float and stand with the most incredible dignity and nobility. There seems to be a simultaneous obeying and defying of the law of gravity. I decided that one of the dolmens was my personal magic carpet. And if one could find one's way onto the magic carpet, one could go anywhere.

QUESTION: Can you say something about what it felt like, and how you prepared yourself, to take these photographs?

CAPONIGRO: Yes, I can say. That decision to pay less attention to being a photographer and more attention to remaining open to what wants to be recorded for what particular purpose —that's too broad; but the stones affected me so much that I dropped my equipment and turned my ear, hoping that I could receive what it was they were trying to tell me. They are very much alive. I had to go through a process of understanding myself to such a degree that I could discern, who says I should make this picture? Will it work? What is it I'm trying to project? I mean all of this was going on at once, and over a long period of time. Now I can speak about it and see that I had to be there in a very definite way, and that I had to understand something about myself. The craft had been worked out to a large extent, that wasn't too much of a problem; but whose thoughts were these? How did I arrive in front of this group of stones? Why this arrangement? And why this play of light?

There were very definite times when I could sense that I was making a picture that I already knew how to make. I had been given a reputation, I'd been given a name that said, "Mr. Caponigro, you're a photographer, and don't let anybody tell you otherwise." And I had to push that aside and ask the stones was it all right to take this picture. They would very often tell me that I could go have a cup of coffee because that wasn't it. That was coming from my fabrication, my ability to manipulate for a purpose that belongs to quite another world. I was trying to get behind those stones. I wanted to hear the voice of the stone, so it took me a while to find out that I also had to learn to be silent and really listen. In that way I could separate my own internal dialogue and the dialogue that was actually taking place between myself and that place. I had to put myself in the middle, in neutral, and wait and hope that I could discern that it was coming from that special place and not from something I had already learned which was telling me, "Don't worry about a thing, you've got it made."

QUESTION: You used the word *eternal,* and for the first time I connected that with human endeavors. I have a feeling that Stonehenge doesn't have the kind of limitations that we face in ourselves, that possibly part of it was built two thousand years later than the first part, which meant a kind of continuation of efforts through that many years, possibly, the passing down of some understanding. It's as though—this almost sounds irreverant—but when I look at Stonehenge, there's lots of sinning.

CAPONIGRO: You didn't get to talk to the head architect. . . .

QUESTIONER: I don't know that it's necessary. . . .

CAPONIGRO: I very much agree with what you said, because I came to that also. You know, they've been talking and writing for years about the mystery of Stonehenge, as if they're going to crack it. What I came to was that they will not crack that mystery, because that mystery is unsolvable. There is that absolute timelessness, and it will persist and still does. And there's a certain amount of force gone from those stones which was provided by certain individuals, our ancestors, who used it in a certain way. But in some unique way that architect, that head architect I'm talking about, placed it just so, and the effect, if one could be open and quiet enough to be in the presence of it, would be a sense that he was telling you something important. He did it in just that way to keep that incredible something that persists eternally.

QUESTION: One of our dilemmas has to do with the disillusionment that people are feeling with the idea that you can find meaning outside yourself, in what is external. Does one have to have the "out there" of a power place or Stonehenge, or even of a craft like photography, to find this very intensely human struggle?

CAPONIGRO: My personal experience was that I had to meet the "out there." I had to prepare myself for the possibility of receiving what it had to say. I watched thousands of people mill in and out of that place. Very few of them stopped. Very few of them looked long enough or hard enough to be affected. I think you have to concentrate in more than one way in order to receive what *is* out there. There's got to be some preparation for the receiving. That trilogy of stones, the preparation people went through: First of all, overcoming, they separate themselves from the world, overcome through this first mound, which is terrifying; then they move on to a second place, which in another sense might purify much more on an emotional level; and then this other place that you can reach, reflected in the third mound. That's a sequence of preparations.

QUESTION: But then is one bound to a place or may one learn their experiences in any life conditions?

CAPONIGRO: Stonehenge is written on every face in this audience. It's on the third floor as well as on the fourth floor. It's in the street. It's on those canvases, on the walls, in one degree or another. Very often it's quite dispersed, but it's not limited to any special place. Man does not recognize the problem of getting to that special place within himself.

QUESTION: How do you solve that problem?

CAPONIGRO: Well, first I have to cut this long umbilical cord that's been attached to me. I don't know how you get through there. First, the interest—if that interest can be sustained, some form of concentration must exist. I took an interest in photography. I realized that I could learn, that it would take me to certain places, that it would give me something to stand on. I didn't have to slip here and there. I didn't have to send my pictures to the drugstore. No, I kept it all in this room, and I went through the whole process, and I discovered that something of quality, some character, could come out of this if I would stay here and follow through. So there's got to be a certain kind of persistence. The other problem in photography is the variables—there are all kinds of problems, the emulsions change, there are problems with the papers, the developers can't be mixed exactly the same—all of that, that's life. The variables—it's there always, banana peels everywhere. You simply have to remember that you are going somewhere and get up and continue.

QUESTION: I was so struck by an extraordinary sense of movement in these stones—a real movement, like they were actually dancing. In the practice of a craft, in a framework of more quiet, there is an opportunity to discover some of that same movement I was able to experience in those pictures. Now somebody living today that doesn't have a craft, doesn't have the opportunity to have those kinds of disciplined, quiet times when you can be doing something, how could that person come to that sense of movement?

CAPONIGRO: Are you a dancer?

QUESTION: No. I make films.

CAPONIGRO: That explains your question. I was feeling a very different movement. I think you are trying to make a movie of it. Your mind would naturally think in terms of a sequence of movements. These stones are stationary, absolutely still. You see maybe five of those massive stones, and you're hopping from one to the next. You're creating the movement in your mind.

QUESTION: The inscriptions on the stones to me were a mirror of the kind of movement that I felt. It is as though they were caught in movement.

CAPONIGRO: Nothing is still. Absolutely nothing stands still, and those stones do vibrate. They are in movement. They have a much greater span of time to go through, for their particular dance, and that is a good way of putting it. They are dancing. That was pretty much what I was after, to sense their internal activity. And there is a lot to be said for the plastic arts, still photography, painting. There is an experience you can have which can suggest to you that there is a place within that is constantly alive, not necessarily moving as such, but constantly alive to how this whole structure is put together. I expressed it a little bit in my early photographs, trying to sense the forces in nature, trying to catch what doesn't move from here to there. Is there a progression? I do sense that something is moving. The creative process—the very creation—is dynamic. So I could see how one of those circles or spirals inscribed on those stones could be in a sense a movement. The idea is movement.

QUESTION: In your own creative process, are you going to move on to something else?

CAPONIGRO: I was in England last August and photographed a few stones that I hadn't photographed before. I got something from the earth on which the stones were standing. I have a feeling I'll investigate the earth to some degree. But I think that the stones will be photographed for some years to come.

QUESTION: One of the themes that I am impressed with in this series of talks is the speed with which things are happening now. I was wondering how your work has helped you face the problems of today. Is there an analogy?

CAPONIGRO: Let us say you're a record, a recording. Years ago we used to have 78 rpm, and then they shifted to 45 rpm. Now we have 33 1/3. We are all records, and time has given us endless recordings. One goes at that speed, and one goes at another speed. But there is a spindle; there's a spindle in man, and the record is placed on that spindle. And that spindle is stationary. It has movement, but it has a place that it does not lose its sense of, and the rest goes round and round. It is also a little like a pendulum clock. We experience difficulty and we experience ecstacy as human beings, and all the grades in between. We are attached to rods that control that movement. There is a point at which it is stationary. There's all this movement like a spiral—upward, downward—but it's that one stationary point that I'm really interested in.

QUESTION: Do you say that these stones can get you to the center?

CAPONIGRO: It is the center that gets you to the center, and I'll go after anything that reminds me about the center—anything, stones, or what's your rpm, whatever.

Hassan Fathy

Hassan Fathy, *author of* Architecture for the Poor, *is a Cairo architect whose life was completely changed when he visited a village on the Upper Nile; in one moment of revelation he saw there "a way of building that was a natural growth in the landscape, as much a part of it as the palm tree." Since then his work in Egypt and elsewhere has had widespread impact, particularly in the developing nations, as a pioneering turn from modern technology toward traditional forms of building and living.*

IF WE WANT to talk about culture, we want to talk about an architecture for the people. But first we have to talk a little about architecture itself, which I think is the most important element of culture. It envelops man. Man lives and is formed by architecture. To my mind the true house is like the shell of a snail. The soft living body of the snail secretes calcium carbonates, and by the action of physical forces these molecules arrange themselves in a spiral form, which becomes a shell. But once the dead and calcified part is created, it in turn acts on the living soft part which created it and gives it form. In a similar process the city shapes the spirit of the community, and architecture becomes one of its most important elements.

The best definition I know of culture is that it is the outcome of the interaction between the intelligence of man and his environment in satisfying both his spiritual and physical needs. We can recognize this interaction in the plastic arts, and it is the real basis of the art of living. Critics and historians of art have created two categories of art, one they call *imitative arts,* which are painting and sculpture, and the other they call the *abstract arts,* which are music and architecture. In my opinion we can not apply such a dogmatic division. If painting were just imitation of nature, a simple recording without applied intelligence, it would be like a photograph. I am not debasing photography, which has become an art in itself, but I mean to say that it would not be painting. And if the abstract arts were devoid of any human reference, music would be just vibrations or sound physics, and architecture would be just engineering.

We have taken technology as being intelligence in interaction with the environment, but the world as the arena of man's spiritual and physical needs has been facing drastic changes since the industrial revolution, especially in what we call the Third World. We know that now the annual income per capita in the Third World varies between fifty and sixty dollars. Nothing can explain such people being alive, living on that amount, unless we remember they have a long history of living outside the cash economy. Now they are being forced into the cash economy before they are ready, before they have enough cash. The people over the centuries have produced an architecture, a cultural base of their own, and now they are dropping it and getting lost. Their own architecture developed out of their way of life and depended on cooperation. The socioeconomic change has affected these poor countries terribly. They are especially handicapped in the field of architecture, of housing, because this requires a high cash outlay. According to United Nations' statistics of fifteen years ago, there were something like eight hundred million who were doomed to a premature death because of bad housing conditions alone, not to speak about nutrition and other needs of life.

So here there is this huge number, which must by now have

surpassed a billion due to the population growth, and the cultural and economic changes have made these people what I call the *economically untouchables.* There are no means of helping these people the way we are practicing architecture in the modern sense, because such people cannot hire an architect to design a house for them nor hire a contractor to build for them. And no government in the world can build for a billion. So this is a critical situation because these economically untouchables represent political trouble. I am sure that the government or the institution that would come with love to help these billion would win them by construction not destruction of their culture, as has been happening in modern times.

This is the most important thing that I wanted to speak to you about, but I would also like to speak to you of the architecture of the people of my country and to express something of the cultural change that has taken place and the effect that it had on my people.

We spoke about culture as the interaction between the intelligence of man and his environment. But what is this environment? It is everything that surrounds man, which is really two environments. There is the God-made environment, which is the landscape with its constituents—mountain, valley, plain, climate, fauna, flora, man himself. If the architect does not respect this environment, we consider this to be a sin against God, because man is the only animal that has the possibility of imposing his structures, his creation, next to God's. And then there is the other environment, the man-made environment, the built environment, the urban environment. We believe that one must respect this one, too, because of those who preceded us who would have respected the first, the God-made environment.

In the past, man was more conscious of the Cosmos than we are today, and we can see how the environment affected man and the architecture. Take the Corinthian column—the Greeks chose the acanthus leaf for the capital because they have the prickly plant in Greece. In Egypt they used the lotus, the papyrus, and even the palm leaf as capital for the columns. But it was not imitation of nature just for imitation; it was for what the acanthus leaf symbolized to the Greeks and what the papyrus and the lotus symbolized to the Egyptians.

Today we are encircled by more of the man-made environment than the God-made. We are surrounded with asphalt roads, concrete, street lamps, and all the mechanical products of our industry. We are cut off almost completely from God's nature. I think that from the beginning—from Adam—the design concept of man was to be in the natural environment surrounded by plants, animals, and everything of the earth, including the atmosphere with its several zones enveloping the earth, the first of which contains the humidity and the air on which all life is feeding. So, it is natural that man's architecture should express his truths in forms related to nature, different areas having different styles.

In India, where plant life is predominant, we can see the resemblance which the Hindu temple has to the cactus plant. And again, when some of the Indians adopted Islam, in their use of the minaret there is seen the form that is almost that of the cactus. This is not simply because they like the plant for its form, as if they were impressionist painters, but for what the plant symbolizes. It represents to them the way of growth—upward, aspiring to the divine—and the way to grow. The cactus breaks the rock and grows out toward the sky.

In Africa, on the contrary, animal life is predominant. There the forms of ears and horns of stags appear, as on a mask, in the architecture. A wall with a doorway will be designed with motifs representing ears, horns, etc., and the door opening will represent the mouth. Beliefs related to animal forces led to this way of decoration. There, the doorway is invested with magic.

This kind of decorated architecture inspired one English architect to animate an otherwise dead facade of a London county council building with a representation, in a most stylized way, of an anthropomorphic mask with the mouth at the doorway. There was no harm in doing that, because it provided an enriching visual experience, but we have in different cultures the interchangeables and the noninterchangeables. When the modern artist put concrete-frame buildings in Nigeria, the Nigerians took this as a sign of progress without questioning. In fact, they scrapped the beautiful sculpture that had inspired the English artist and whitewashed both the new concrete-frame buildings and the old mud brick buildings.

This is a change in culture and could be admitted, but change is never neutral; if it is not for better, it is for worse. This is a change for the worse. Since architecture is one of the most important elements of a whole culture, it should be the role of cultural institutions and organizations like UNESCO to encourage the preservation of indigenous social custom in major architectural projects. Today we have a kind of social change that takes place not by the people but, unfortunately, by the architects in their economic role of builders of whole communities.

A clear example is Nubia in the southern part of Egypt between Aswan and Sudan. It has been sacrificed three times in its history. The first time was when the Aswan Dam was built in 1902, and the whole area was flooded. The second time was in 1934, when there was a second elevation of the dam. During its construction, the people built new homes. The people built an entire region in one year with no architects, no contractors, no lorries, nothing at all to build with except what they had in their hands and under their feet as material, which was mud. The water had risen to one meter from the old houses when they started to move into the new villages they built above. The homes were all mud brick, and the people utilized different forms of decoration and architectural expression, but it was still all symbolic to them in such things as the ears on the sides of the doorways.

What is more important is that they would not have been able to achieve this miracle of construction unless they had both the material, which was clay, and, at the same time, the techniques which they inherited from ancient times, especially the vaulting. Any peasant can build a wall, but when he comes to the roof he is defeated. But they solved this problem from antiquity by having the barrel vault form the shape of a catenary. The continuity of tradition is suggested by the mud house of a man called Amid Adidin that was built in 1934. The latter is almost a copy of a Third Dynasty Palace even to the ventilation holes underneath and the cornice on top. There is something like four thousand years separating the two, but the image has been transmitted, and the knowledge must have been continuing on in a culture, as we said, that is full—invested—with magical forms.

When the new high dam was later constructed at Aswan, the Nubian area was flooded for the third time. This time architects designed the new settlement for the Nubians. We, with available

38

technology, built a downstream village, and the design was that of contemporary architects. For all the buildings the architect designed only one basic model, or it might be four, considering that the same exterior design has two, three, or four rooms. And from this they built in rows seventeen thousand identical attached houses. When the Nubians come home at night—they like to drink and often come home a little tipsy—they have to count the doorways to find which house is theirs. Should they lose count, they have to go back to the beginning and start again. When compared to what the Nubians had before, this kind of architectural or cultural revolution is dehumanizing because it is not sensitive to nature. It is not needed.

Unfortunately, the Nubians soon became like the Nigerians, preferring the concrete structures. After I had been asked to design a new village in Aswan for the Nubians, I found that they wanted the concrete. I talked with them and showed them what they had done for themselves and what been done by others for them. They became convinced that they would like to come back to their own traditional architecture. But the final decision was not based only on our feelings and photographic material. We had a group of ten graduate students from London University come and evaluate nine models of homes that we had constructed in Cairo which varied in construction from completely mud brick to completely prefabricated concrete. Air temperature in April was $17°$ Celsius ($30.6°$F) higher in the prefabricated concrete model than in the mud brick. And we call the mud brick "backward" and the concrete "progressive technology." This is a misuse of the word *technology.*

With the return to the mud brick technology, what has happened to the traditional decoration? I say that prior to the last flooding of the region, Nubia surpassed Iphigenia. But it did not have the fate of Iphigenia, although it sacrificed itself three times. Iphigenia sacrificed herself once, when the oracle said to Agamemnon that she had to be sacrificed. And the gods saved her. Nubia has been saved, but what did they do to their own mud brick houses? They are decorated, but now when we have schools in Nubia and the art masters come from Cairo to teach, their effect on the indigenous art produces a decoration which lacks the force of the Nubian's own native magic. And the gods do not save them. This is decadence. What is native is called backward, but when they are progressive, this is what happens to them. You see, this is what is happening in every sense to these countries, and nobody is preserving cultural values and the art of living.

We can compare an interior of an old house in Nubia and one of the new houses that has almost the same form. There is a similarity because of the form, and the form springs out of the same essential forces. In the decoration we can see the differences in quality, as when a man goes to a psychiatrist and the psychiatrist makes him scribble on paper so he can analyze his personality. What we are speaking about is form and the effect of land; I mean the effect of nature on a people and the lines they choose. In a simple way we find the same curve in the cactus, in a turban, and in the dome. This selective quality is something inherent in the race which we are forgetting about.

When we architects design, we design mostly on blank paper as if we were putting our buildings in the interstellar space. But when we build, we find a difference—that the building does not work there, and even that the building does not express properly. It is a costume designed by a decorator not a costume for the ballet. But the functional requirements for the ballet are so exacting that the costume, in order to be made and used, may have nothing of the original design. What guides the design of a mud brick house when the architect wants to step into the field of folk art? I say that folk art comes from the genius of the race; high art is from the disciplined expression of the individual artist. We have the Apollonian art and the Dionysian. And when Apollo wants to step into the field of Dionysus, he has to be very careful not to try to imitate because, as in much folk art, the importance comes—almost—from the imperfections that follow the humor of the artist. And if we come and make it very straight and regular, with compasses, etc., it loses its quality and becomes bad workmanship; I mean without character. Not to imitate does not mean to reject the old forms as invalid. If one studies traditions to try to understand, one can come again to an expression of form that is living. There are examples, still, where a beauty is created from starting at the beginning with valuing the demands imposed by simple construction techniques.

In the fourth century, when the Christians were leaving Rome for the desert, they too had no lorries, no contractors, no cement —nothing but the desert. But they built themselves 250 shrines and houses and tombs which are still standing. Interesting as history, but no architect has ever gone to really look, to evaluate and assess the potential that is there. In many ways the poor people are like the oasis. They are cut off from any participation in the system which is based on cash economy, and the architect neglects to assess and adapt the old cultural values that created the forms in their lives. These values developed the vault and dome techniques that solved the problem of roofing. Today the form seems to occur only in a few places, such as Iran and Nubia, and the technique is dying out in both countries. We are losing the beauty that we can get from space created by these forms. Space, today, with efficient technology, becomes rectangular, simple, and horizontal, with a flat roof. It does not have the beauty of lines going up and down molding an integral space. When the dome or arch is structural, the beauty comes automatically; the beauty comes from the form and the forces that are acting on it. The form could not be otherwise; it would collapse. So the form is forcibly beautiful.

Similarly, the forces of nature have created desert architecture and a cultural form. The desert is hostile to man, so he built his houses to shut himself off completely from the outside, to open inward. All the old houses were introverted because one sensibly limits exposure to the outside. It is different in Europe or California where the landscape is beautiful, and it would be unwise to shut oneself off from this beauty. This Western world cultural influence, however, is being felt in Saudi Arabia and other desert countries. They are rejecting the old forms of the desert. Town planning and architecture in this part of the world were based on this introversion, but now they are changing to extraversion and ruining everything by not respecting the God-made environment.

So what do we have with this cultural revolution? The people are now almost free to design and build whatever they want— they could extend to infinity! But that is why they have been building leisurely, and building has become a leisurely activity. It has become decoration not connected with the forces of their nature.

It reminds me of the story about Einstein when he had a cat. He made a hole in the door, and when the cat had kittens, he opened a smaller hole in the door for the little cats to pass. To know what is needed can elude the most sincere man, but it is imperative that we try to discover those needs.

For example, in one house where we tried to solve problems of household work, there was the question of laundry washing. Traditionally, after washing, the water is thrown into the courtyard in front of the door, and this makes it messy. So, we built in an area that was sunken. The position was calculated exactly so as to give the best situation for the muscles for the man or the woman who washes so that after the laundry washing was finished, all that had to be done was to tip over the basin and the water drained into a hole. And it worked for ten years, keeping the courtyard bone dry. But when the owner left the house and it was occupied by some other fellow, he used the sunken area for storage; he did not know what it was for.

It is still the details that are important. When we built a market, instead of the usual marketplace where the vendors have their goods and wares on the ground under the heat of the sun, we built a canopy over the area and, in front, we even planted trees to shade the cattle.

But most important is where people live and the sense of community. When I designed a village, I tried to arrange the space so as not to have the gridiron pattern but to divide it into neighborhoods of fifteen to twenty families together. We built their houses around a private square or courtyard, so that when they came out of their houses they would not immediately become anonymous in the impersonal life of the village itself. It would be gradual. They have their courtyards in the house, and they come into an area which is a street but not a thoroughfare—a walkway with a bend and, perhaps, a little arch window as a focal point, where a man can greet a friend.

This was the form; I left the decoration to the people. And they did decorate. Around one doorway, for instance, there were symbols of the earth, a star, and the goddess of the sky. I asked about it, and the Nubian said, "Oh, it is for the bad eye." So you see, it is hieroglyphic, pure hieroglyphic. But it survives because superstition survives religion. When the old religious knowledge is lost, the forms continue as superstition. In a sense, this is culture.

Today we architects are yet another step removed. There is little to connect us to the folk architecture, but we have something, the sensibilities to transpose—not to imitate; that would be wrong. I cannot imitate the humor of the peasant. To transpose means to look and then to try to find the origin of the forces, the understanding, in myself. When I build a house for a peasant, I build it for myself, the peasant. When I build a house for a prince, I build it for myself, the prince. An artist should never reduce the quality of his design, his search; he has to meet with the best in himself. It is like music; every musician is beating his own record in every composition, as we can see if we follow the sequence of compositions by Brahms or Beethoven.

To transpose must also include looking at the broader world view, including the cultural revolution. People will say, "You are not contemporary; you are using mud; you are turning back in time, in history." But to my mind it is necessary to define well what we mean by modern, what is contemporary. When we look at the dictionary, the meaning of the word *contemporary* is living or occurring at the same time. So we have two things parallel— Napoleon was contemporary with Nelson—but it does not carry any value judgment. For the ancients to achieve this contemporaneity, they designed their temples parallel to the order of the cosmos. When the earth was under the sign of the Twins, they designed their temple to coincide with the sky, the astronomical arrangement, in angles and dimensions and all other aspects. When the earth moved to the sign of the Bull, they dismantled the temple and rebuilt it on the same site to coincide with the new conditions. So they achieved contemporaneity that way.

But the temple was one single building whose purpose related to the cosmos. What are we to do when we want to achieve contemporaneity in our modern architecture? What is our standard of reference for housing people? If we want our buildings to be contemporary, probably we have to make our buildings fit with the latest findings of modern science. We have made great progress in the physical and mechanical sciences, but we have made much less in the human sciences, the science of the human being. If we could widen our understanding and apply this to our planning and design, we could reach the same sanctity of the temple in our buildings and in our cities because they would be designed for man incarnating the microcosmos—man-microcosm. In that way we can achieve contemporaneity.

The development of the physical and mechanical sciences without equivalent discoveries in the human sciences has produced a technology that allows buildings without any human reference whatsoever. From this anonymity there is a fear of change that is taking place in America. In the very beginning when they first started the highrise, the freedom was exciting and, superimposed on the structures were reminiscences of the renaissance that could be related to. But technology progressed, and it was found that light-weight glass could be used for whole exteriors, which increased the freedom to build even bigger buildings. We have been freed of imitation and associations with past cultures, but I think that, with the glass building, we lost all connection with nature; we eliminated man—and, maybe, architecture itself, if we consider architecture as space enclosed within walls for man's physical and spiritual needs. With glass walls architecture will seep out; it will not be enclosed. And compare the reflection of glass with the Indian temple where every millimeter is carved with qualities of man. You know the story of the man passing by three people dressing stone. And he asks the first one, "What are you doing?" He said, "I am earning my living." He asked the second, "And you?" And he said, "I am dressing a stone." When he asked the third, "And you, what are you doing?" he said, "I am building a cathedral." There is a great difference among the three. To my mind, we are not even dressing stone because we have no stone to dress now. We have fabricated glass; we have a whole wall hanging like a miniskirt. That is our reference to man.

In architecture, when we consider the human reference, I look at a temple like the Parthenon. They say that Greek temples are the architecture of humanism. The Doric is the masculine. The column is carrying the entablature with strength in a good proportion. I can judge with my feelings—although I did not carry the stone—that the proportions of the entablature as weight is proportionate to the column. We could ascertain the strengths and resistances of our material at a laboratory and build a column of half the size, but it would not be beautiful in the same way. So it is more than mechanical; it is human reference by which we are judging the beauty. We are taking the part of the column, incarnating the column, substituting the column by man. In the same way they say that the Ionic order is feminine, because its proportions are more delicate than the sturdy Doric. They even had the caryatids, where they removed the columns and put in sculptured figures of women.

Another idea of human reference in architecture is the Temple of Ammon at Luxor. It was begun by Amenophis III and was completed by Ramses II, two hundred years later. They projected man-microcosm onto the plan of the temple. The temple was designed in its entirety to represent man in his entirety. The covered temple represented the head of this man-microcosm and, at each stage of construction, represented not only a portion of the body but also represented stages of growth in the life of man. It was built in stages, and at every stage it had human reference and contemporaneity.

Today we are in great need of returning as men to our decisions, because we have eliminated the human scale in our buildings, the aesthetic factor, the human reference. It is not enough to have buildings properly proportioned and beautiful as an abstract design; they must be related to man. To my mind the touchstone of the veracity of the value of any project lies in the answer to the question, is it for man or something else? If it is for man, then we have something to discuss; but if it is for something else, like economy or politics, then anything could be done—there is no constraint whatsoever—but we shall fall back into chaos not into Cosmos.

QUESTION: You talked about the effects of technology on the primitive society, and we begin to see the effects of technology on our society as well. For example, you spoke of people who have to be taught again to use their own indigenous architecture; we have mothers who have to be taught again to breastfeed their children. What is it from your point of view that creates the effect that technology has on us? How can it be that this what-we-call technology has such a deleterious effect on these people and also on ourselves?

FATHY: It is not technology as such because technology is neutral. It is what we do with technology. According to the dictionary definition, technology is all that concerns the use of science for commercial purposes. So technology can be directed toward the interests of the producer and the consumer. But how can we resist what we do with technology? It is very difficult to resist any facility. Man does not understand that, for every facility in his life, his life loses a lot. What matters is the process not the result. What is a man doing when he dresses a stone? He is removing the superfluous and leaving the essential; he is spiritualizing the stone and is spiritualizing himself, too. But I discount the value of this when I take the facility, let us say, of concrete. I am not against concrete because it has important uses, but it is an example that shows the difference between men manipulating one material and another. Concrete needs a third-class carpenter to nail flat planks to make forms and a third-class blacksmith to bend rods and pour concrete.

What is the experience of man with materials? Concrete has released construction from the constraints of material, but man is not released by removing constraints. We have to understand freedom through constraint not through every new facility. To my mind a city is not the buildings, streets, etc.; it is the million acts that go into its making and the million acts that are going on within the city at every moment. I tried once to evaluate just those acts that go into the building of the city. We have the creative flavor—the architect, the planner; we have the technical knowledge—the engineer, the special engineer, the roads engineer; and we have the builders—the administrative, the skilled labor, the unskilled labor. Then I took the qualities needed for every decision made by each one of them—what it would give as quality in man. By what we have we can qualitatively evaluate the loss and gain in human values, in human quality. If we want to bring out the human values, it might be that we can come back on our decisions and not rush to take any facility. The ancients knew certain facilities, but they never allowed themselves to fall into this.

But now we have answers to so many problems, and we take the first answer; we take the formulation of the problem for granted, without question. If, for example, I have a geographic area and I am asked to put so many people there, I have the facility to do it. But there is an optimum distribution of people that I can put on a geographical area; if I increase, I would be reducing something of the quality of life for these people. It is exactly as if I have a glass with a 50cc volume; I cannot put in 51. It would spill out. But when I am forced, and they ask me to do it, I can —and I am glad because I can do it. I will freeze the water, and I can put 1000cc in a column.

But if I apply this to buildings, I will be freezing something in man. We haven't considered man properly yet. Man is in great need of being in contact with Mother Earth because there are fluids and radiations coming from the ground that support life. I always think of the contrast when I think of the quality of life. Take a house in one of the Greek islands. The house has two rooms; it might be thirty or forty square meters all in all, but it has two thousand square meters in front where the children and the grownups can stay and enjoy life. If I put them on the tenth floor even, not the hundredth, I will cut them off from the two thousand square meters they used to enjoy when they were on Mother Earth. So I think that we ought to introduce into our planning the encounters with plants and animals, because man was created within the natural environment. When man is deprived of the plants, he has the flowerpots that he puts on his balcony, and dogs and cats to have this company of man. This is really needed, you know!

There are solutions to all these problems of density and distribution over the surface of the earth, the geographic area we are occupying, that include man. There is not only the highrise; we can also spread out. The Greeks, when the community exceeded twenty thousand, I think, had a new colony. In cities we can have the same articulation without spreading too much, as we have in Los Angeles. By articulating, we start with the unit because by this we have recourse to what we have learned from our physique, our bodies. I see that my finger is composed of three joints. Between two is a unit in my finger that is a system to the cells that compose it. As I grow, each unit has its ecological balance of the cells of skin and bones and blood and everything. So here we have our basis of planning.

If we want to increase, we also have to recognize that we have ranges and limits beyond which we cannot grow. If we arbitrarily increase an animal like the mouse by three times, he will not live because we are increasing the weight by the cube of the linear dimension, and we lose the inner balance of the mouse. The heaviest land animal, they say, is the elephant. He weighs, I think, three to five thousand pounds; but when he goes into the water and becomes a whale, he can grow to 30,000. Here he will have another limitation—he cannot grow indefinitely—which is the heart. He would need subsidiary hearts to pump the blood into all the veins.

So you see, we have to think about what we are doing in every decision; we should not take the first idea. We have to consider all the factors that can occur to man, not only for now but also for the future. We have to try to extend our thinking toward the ultimate aim of man, of life on earth. We cannot stop. We have this movement of urbanization, which is, to my mind, like the gregarious instinct. It is like the cells coming together. Do they find organically, physiologically, biologically, that they can resist the environment better? They come together, and that is why we have the species. Nature is very kind. We have the possibility of an interaction of intelligence with the environment, but, overall, she makes us do what she wants us to do—kill one another, even, to achieve what she wants. She has the nearer aims and the further aims. Let us take flirtation as a nearer aim to a further aim, marriage; marriage, a nearer aim to a further aim, procreation; procreation, a nearer aim to a further aim, propogation of the race; propogation of the race, a nearer aim to a further aim, continuity of life; continuity of life, a nearer aim to a further aim, evolution. Evolution is a nearer aim to what further aim? Here we stop!

If we try to situate man in life in general, in the vast universal setting of things, I think we can solve immediate problems in a more humane way. The worst thing to do for a community is to give it a town or a city overnight, because it is in the building wherein lie the motivations for culture. The value is in the evolution, in movement—this kind of revelation of self by having, dealing, and grabbing at nature and stone and marble and wood.

In France, now, they have revived the movement called the *compagnonnage,* companions, which began in the Middle Ages, and they are trying to reintroduce these values, these human values. Did you know that, when they were building a cathedral, the workshop was exactly like the plan of the cathedral, and the workmen and draftsmen were sitting around in an order, as in a religious service, and chanting, so that every movement, every muscle, would be radiating the spirit they were putting into it. And as spectators, if we were allowed in, we would feel it without knowing it, as if we were in a cathedral like Chartes or Notre Dame.

These are real values; I think that this is the problem that we have set for ourselves. How to come back on our decisions? How to bring back the human scale, aesthetics, spirituality even? We have lost contact with nature. To bring back this environment would be fantastic. But I know it is idealistic—too much so; it does not seem practical now—but if we set a problem, to my mind formulating the problem is 90 percent of the solution, at least.

QUESTION: What is the effect on man of shooting him into outer space? They are even talking about having colonies and cities in space. What effect do you think that will have?

FATHY: The only thing that interested me in man reaching the moon in these rockets was that he had to have his breakfast of egg and bacon. We have the man and his nature, he cannot get out of it, and, certainly, to live outside this space will not be enough. I am not a physician, but to my limited knowledge we are affected by the cosmic rays—plants even are affected by these cosmic rays —and if I change this environment, this relationship to the cosmic rays coming from the outside, it would affect my body. Our design concept is that we are supposed to live on the crust of the earth. We have some tolerance. When these astronauts go high up, they are covered with these big masks with the pressure controlled and with the oxygen. But we cannot have this in common life—children having to play with these masks—and if it comes off, you die immediately. I think that we have to consider what our design concept is, and we have to respect it. Every deviation, every change that we make in our surroundings will have an effect on our body, not to mention our psyche.

QUESTION: Once, while visiting Bokhara, a city of beautiful buildings, I also noticed two children that had to wait about twenty minutes to fill a bucket of water, and then they had to carry that bucket about a quarter of a mile back to their home. Would it be consistent with your vision of living well to make use of technological options, such as, in Bokhara, to have a modern water system? Do we still have a certain obligation to use our best tools to create more energy, better communication, refrigeration, as part of a better world? Is quality of living inconsistent with the use of the latest and best practices and options of modern technology?

FATHY: No, they are not against quality as such. There are fields where technology is applicable. We have to give to God what belongs to God and to Caesar what belongs to Caesar. When we come to man, he belongs to God. But for the facilities we have options. There are ways and means of reaching the water from a distance; we can make it even beautiful. We can make a canal meandering and have a park around. We can solve the problem if we set it properly; we can solve the problem of facilities. I am not against technology, but we have to subject technology to human values, to the economy of man. I spoke about technology as I did because we have made bad use of technology—as we said about buildings. Now we are having this billion homeless or with bad housing. There is technology for the Bedouin or the Masai which is different from the technology for the Londoner or the Parisian or the New Yorker. Technology has no character; it's what can be done with it. We have to know where to apply it. There are ways and means of using this technology for beautifying life, but not the way we have been doing it, polluting the environment, having all the facilities with no thinking whatsoever. Even here, you are beginning; you refuse to have the Concorde flying because it would change something with the ozone and affect the atmosphere. The Concorde is a facility—the technology of coming across the Atlantic in three hours—but what effect can it have on the atmosphere and the stratosphere and the substratosphere and, eventually, each one of us. We have just not to take anything easily without thinking; we have to see the chain reaction to its last repercussion.

QUESTION: Can you say something about the different units of physical measuring systems of different cultures and how these different systems are related to man's body? How does adopting one or another affect human movement through space or human life in general?

FATHY: This is an interesting question because space is defined—the different spaces—by lines. But if we take vision, the eye does not see more than a point at a time on a line. The eye goes point after point and sends each experience to the brain; like music, we feel note after note, and we compose the melody in the brain. So I have introduced rhythm in my movement. If this movement were rhythmic, harmonic, it would be pleasing, especially if I could subdivide. The distance I have to go is then related. This is the human reference that we were talking about. When I walk, if I measure the distance by my measurements, I am not making an abstraction of man, I am measuring by the foot, by the cubit, and so on. These are human measurements, and I can subdivide subconsciously and feel the movements were harmonic. I mean to say that the musical distance, the proportions— four, three, five, etc.—would be pleasing because the eye would be moving musically. But if I can relate this movement to me, it becomes more human. It would be not simply pure rhythm; it would be human rhythm, too. So I regret that we are going to the metric system, making an abstraction of me, of man.

QUESTION: Let us suppose that the long-awaited San Francisco earthquake has come and destroyed the city. If you were commissioned to plan out a new city for us, what sort of buildings, of structure, would you recommend for our lives?

FATHY: Let us put the question differently. Suppose, now, that we discovered America today. What sort of cities would we build; what would we do with America, in this case, if man were to react with this environment, be respectful of this environment? The house is not just shaped from the atmosphere. Can we find a standard of reference? What would be truth, true to what? Truth to this environment would be to the materials that are available here, to the climate, to every aspect or element that composes this environment. But we have to consider another thing—that we have architecture and town planning. Architecture is a communal art, and it could not spring up overnight. It is not the expression of an individual. That is the problem with our cultural change that is taking place now. We are arbitrary when we discard the traditional without analysis, without even the wish to understand. But if we were to start anew here in this part of the world with a new architecture, what would it be? If we have not any past experience, we shall be depending entirely upon school knowledge, which is not enough, to my mind, because there are cycles of evolution, of interaction with the environment, that need more than one life span experience, but which are communicated by tradition. When I chase a fly, I do not think; I do it automatically, by instinct. If I were to do it consciously, I would first learn all the diseases it can transmit to me. But the fly would have been gone for miles.

So here the question is very interesting because this is what we have to do to come to an answer. We set all the buildings that are to be put up in San Francisco, or any city, and we have to find some sort of basic and fundamental standard of reference. What would be the truth, the form to fit into this part of the world together with the society, with the community? We should not allow what is now happening to be a determinant in our design. We have to think of what should be happening not what has been happening. You have had in this part of the world something like the Spanish Moorish style. From an aesthetic point of view it would fit into the climate, but we cannot have an imitation like that. Even if it did spread here because of a similar climate, it might not be fitting in this part of the world if you consider other factors. These are the problems with which we have to work our minds, but it might be two hundred years trying to answer this question by a set of researches and very qualified architects with sensitivity, working one generation after another, to show what nature might have introduced normally with an evolution of culture over five thousand years, more or less. With us the problem is that we have so many facilities of knowledge about structures and about function and about design, but they are not all there is. We do not know nature.

Take the sacred architecture, the building of new churches and cathedrals. We compare them with the old ones, and we feel, when we think about the feeling of the sacred, that there is a big difference between the modern and the old ones. Why? Is it different because it is old? It is because of what went into it, like the sculptor when he is feeling the clay he is modeling—putting energy into the clay—and then the clay really radiates the energy he put in. This we would find in monasteries; all that the monks put in by faith would be there; you would feel it. But once in a monastery I saw a row of ten concrete rooms. I told the bishop, "My dear father, what have you done to your monastery? These are like a set of rooms for servants in a third-class hotel in Cairo." And he agreed. He said, "That is because they had an architect who graduated from school not a monk."

We would wish the sage with his revealed knowledge to regard man and his materials. If they were the Sufi and the companions, the one with his revealed knowledge and the other the craftsman with his skilled hands, together they create these masterpieces. Now we have the architect-contractor, and see what is being done. I think we have to have architects work like the companions on the job and not to limit everything to drafting, because never in history were drafting instruments a determinant in architectural style. We know that climate and materials are determinants of style, but now the T-square has become the determinant of modern architecture.

I think that what you said, the question of starting anew, has helped us to think. We have to find the core of the problem, and then we will find the means. It will take time, it cannot be done overnight, because we have to return then to the craftsmen of the crafts system and the wisdom of the ancients and of evolution. Some architects are learning about, and I am personally interested in, the *Companion* line. I have read most of the books written, and there is only one dealing with the actual building. It is the book of prayers for the master mason who built the Abbey of Le Thoronet in the south of France. He is describing the mathematics, the harmonics that they applied to his plan, and then he talks about the symbols of mercury and gold, among other things. You read it and you say, what is the architecture, where does it apply? But after you have read this, you find yourself with a new vision which comes through what we have been cut off from. If we just learn about this, the symbolic value of all that is surrounding man, not only metals but the stars and so on, we will find that we have a new vision opening a new field for us.

QUESTION: Do you think it would be possible in the present day to build a concert hall the way it was fifty years ago?

FATHY: We have constants, and we have transposition and change. There are constants we should keep, if it be from fifty years ago or even a hundred years ago. When they first built the concert hall in Paris, I was a student and I went to see it. I was a music lover. I took one of the best seats, but it was in some sort of limited gallery; it was like television. I could see the orchestra beautifully, but I wanted to see the audience. When they criticize Albert Hall in London, it is because of the acoustics—and they could be better—but you can see everybody. To my mind, the audience and the effect of music on them is a great part of the enjoyment because music is supposed to be for the audience. Why does a musician compose? It is to have the approval of his fellow kinsmen, to make sure that they approve of his existence. When I am at a concert, there are passages that pass in the music, and it affects me. If I look at my neighbor and I find that he is looking at me at the same time, he would be closer to me because I know he has been having the same feelings as myself. We become very close, and we do not have many chances to come close to one another. So I would design a concert hall like Albert Hall, which I think was built more than fifty years ago. I would correct for the acoustics, but I would keep the feeling of oneness of the community—of becoming one with the community—because sound is something, but so is the audience. I would like music to feel like it is a social thing, as when you go to the opera. The ladies, in the past, used to make dresses to show off when they went to the opera. There are certain things in design we have to respect, and that is the social, people coming together under this uniting, which is beauty in music. It is one of the most civilized actions, and we should never oversimplify any of these factors. We should never be concerned simply with acoustics. I would like to have the background to show off the ladies. I would never like to have them pass against a concrete wall, or something gray. I would like it to be very delicate and matching . . . adding and making it a composition. I would put the audience as a factor in my design at every step.

QUESTION: Is there something in our present economic situation, which is a cash economy, that would prevent the sort of humanization of life or the fulfillment of life that you spoke of . . . the sort of life you project for, say, a people building from their own resources, their own tradition?

FATHY: Yes! But now I say that nothing should. I think that if we are responsible as architects we cannot go against man for any reason—economics, politics, whatever it is. So this is what I have to have in mind, because otherwise I will be going against my conscience, my consciousness, and this matters more than anything else, to my mind as an artist.

René Dubos

René Dubos first demonstrated the feasibility of obtaining antibiotics from bacteria forty years ago. He is now associated with Rockefeller University in New York City as Professor Emeritus of Microbiology and Experimental Pathology. He is the author of several widely read books, including the Pulitzer prize–winning So Human an Animal.

AS SOON AS I read the phrase *the art of living,* there came back to my mind some of my early experiences when I was heavily involved in medical research. At what was then the Rockefeller Institute for Medical Research we spoke of the *science* of medicine, and then, with some scorn, we referred also to the *art* of medicine. The science of medicine is the immense body of factual knowledge scientists have been accumulating for two thousand years. The art of medicine is something very different. It consists in attempting to use that body of knowledge; then, finding that it usually is not sufficient to understand the condition of the patient, the physician comes in with his intuitions, his vague understanding of human nature, his experience dealing with human beings, and practices the *art* of medicine. Well, in a way, I think the art of living corresponds to something very similar to the art of medicine. We have a tremendous body of facts about life, but when it comes to living we have to depend upon our intuitions and our judgment. So when I say how difficult it is to provide the art of living through the facts that we know, allow me to quote from a statement by Bernard Shaw. He was very much puzzled by the fact that the healthy and prosperous young adults he saw around him in England early in this century were disenchanted, in fact, very unhappy. This is the way he had it: "They have got enough food. They have sexual freedom and indoor toilets. Why the deuce aren't they happy?" Well, I think this is a marvelous statement of the very puzzling fact that we have created so much comfort for our life and yet are so rarely successful in using all these facilities to practice the art of living.

In one of the other discussions Dr. Needleman raised the question whether it was not the technological world in which we live that is responsible for much of our lack of happiness, our failure to practice successfully the art of living. To some extent I believe he is right in accusing technology. But I believe I have observed that what in technology has been responsible for our collective unhappiness is beginning to change. And perhaps I can illustrate this change by providing a historical example which I witnessed in my early days in this country.

In the year 1933 the city of Chicago celebrated its one-hundredth anniversary with one of the most spectacular world's fairs that was ever held. It was called The Century of Progress. The whole theme of the fair was that progress, improvement, betterment of human life, were *all* due to scientific technology. I secured a guidebook to the fair, and I have kept it all these years because it's so revealing of the state of mind that prevailed all over the Western world in the early 1900s until the 1940s. The guidebook to the fair described all the marvels of scientific technology and then continued, "Human beings, all societies, will fall in step with the creations of scientific technology." And the writer of the guide was so enthused with his theme that he had a final chapter with a title that read as follows: "Science Discovers, Industry Applies, Man Conforms." I dare state that nobody would write that phrase today. It would be considered absolutely unacceptable to state that man must conform to the dictates of technology. And it seems to me that this is where an immense change has begun to take place in public consciousness. Intellectually, at least, we have completely reversed our position. We no longer believe that man must conform to technology; we believe that we must rethink technology to make it conform to all the natural forces, including the forces of the human spirit. And in a way the art of living will consist in attempting not to abandon technology, because we will not do it—even those of us who think we should will not try to do that—but to make it compatible with human life and with the natural world.

In part, the art of living could then depend upon a science of living, just as the art of medicine depends in part upon the science of medicine. And in this case, upon the science of human life, human biology. But, in fact, most biological sciences are concerned with the structures and the mechanisms that make living possible. We have been immensely successful in working out those purely deterministic aspects of living, those that depend upon the operations of our body and of our mind. But living is something above and beyond the operations of our body and of our mind as conditioned by deterministic forces. Living, as I see it, implies using those biological resources to carry out the kind of activities that we want to undertake and also to become what we would like to become. In a peculiar way living implies at every moment some kind of choice. And that kind of choice always seems to go beyond determinism. In fact, for me it is impossible to discuss the art of living if I take a purely deterministic view of life. I don't see any point discussing this theme further if I do not acknowledge that I believe in free will. But that's not such a common state of mind. As you well know, the most famous psychologists of our time do not see any necessity for recognizing free will or its operation, in fact, do not believe that there is any such thing as free will. And I shall immediately acknowledge that there is no evidence, scientific or otherwise, for free will except our experience of free will. If you do not feel yourself endowed with free will, I would advise you to leave this room immediately, were it only to demonstrate that you *have* free will. Concerning free will, I think we have not added anything since a statement made exactly two hundred years ago by Samuel Johnson. It was in 1778: "All science is against free will, but all personal experience is for it." So now I'm going to restate the problems of the art of living in the terms of my personal kind of scientific knowledge, which is chiefly biological. I'm going to divide the art of free will into two really very different classes of experience, the experience of life, which in reality is the experience of the self, what we do with our life, how we act, by attempting to create something somewhat different from us.

About the experience of life, most people are under the illusion that they can be happy only if something especially good happens in the way they use life. Oddly enough, there is only one phrase that I know to express that life is good per se, that just being alive is good. Whenever one wants to say that, one uses the French expression—in all languages; one speaks of *joie de vivre*. *Joie de vivre* simply means that just being alive is an extraordinary experience. It is perhaps the greatest single experience one can have. The quality of that experience anyone can see by watching a young child or a young animal playing in the spring. It is totally immaterial what goes on, except for the fact that one is alive. It does not mean that you are very happy with the way you live; you can even be suffering. You can have lots of trouble, but just being alive is a quality per se. When I searched through the dictionaries to find the reason for the peculiar fact that the phrase *joie de vivre* has been accepted in all languages—try to translate it into English, you'll see how difficult it is—in French literature I could find only one book with that title. It's from a novel written at the end of the last century by the French novelist Emile Zola, and the title is *La Joie de Vivre*. And what is extraordinary about that title is that the hero of that book is a person who is miserable, suffering from all sorts of physical ailments, all sorts of troubles in his family, a very boring life in a boring French village. But then a young woman commits suicide, and when he is told that, this gentleman who is old, who suffers, who can hardly move, says, "How stupid can one be to take one's life. To be alive is such an extraordinary experience."

Now this *joie de vivre*, I believe, is a purely biological experience. It does not depend upon any intellectual apprehension. It depends upon a perception of the totality of existence through one's senses, not at all an intellectual achievement. Many writers have talked around that topic. Albert Schweitzer is quoted often for having written about reverance for life. But in reality, this is a very poor translation of Albert Schweitzer's thought. What impressed him was the fact that life was a force that permeated the whole surface of the earth and gave some kind of quality totally different from that of the rest of creation. Schweitzer was not a scientist, but he had perceived that, if it were not for life, our globe would be as bare, as dull, as the moon has been shown to be, as Mars has been shown to be, and as all the other planets are known to be. There is a peculiar quality to life which has created everything that we find unique about the earth.

Now I'm going to go to another aspect of the art of living which is more peculiar to human beings and which I suspect does not exist as we know it in the rest of animal life. We are naturally animals; we have much in common with all the higher animals. We probably originated as a species somewhere in a somewhat tropical environment of East Africa. Now there is one great difference between the animals that originated in East Africa and the human beings that originated there. All animals, whatever their species, stay within the natural environment in which they have evolved. You can look at the most powerful lion or tiger—it will move a few miles here and there, but it will not change environments. Look at the polar bear—powerful as it is, it will not move from the environment in which it has evolved. But for mysterious reasons, one of the greatest mysteries of human life, we as a species began a hundred thousand years ago to move away from the environment in which we have evolved. We are still biologically the same kind of semitropical animal that we were a hundred thousand years ago when we functioned in East Africa. But instead of remaining in the area in which we had evolved, and to which we are adapted, we elected—Lord knows why—to move away from it and to invade the whole surface of the globe. That is a very peculiar thing to do. No other animal has taken the risks involved in moving away from its natural environment.

We could not move from East Africa—if that's the place where we originated—without taking the most phenomenal kind of risks —risk with regard to the climate, to the kind of food that we would find, risk with regard to the configuration of the environment in which we would have to function. And yet this has been all of human prehistory and history—taking risks, moving away from the biological comfort of the environment in which we evolved. I have recently been visiting professor in one of the largest schools of engineering in this country. And one of the seminars I was asked to manage was called The Acceptability of Risk. The intention was that we would ask technical people to measure the risks involved in any of the technological innovations of our time—measure the risk of developing nuclear energy, of developing this or that kind of chemical, of creating a new physical environment in which we live. Now we know quite well how to do that. Engineers know how to do it. They can tell you statistically the risk to be expected from building a nuclear reactor, from going back to coal for energy, from developing this or that kind of detergent; one knows how to calculate all of that. But oddly enough, our decisions are never made on this kind of calculations.

Our decisions, I believe, are made on something entirely different. We take risks for the sake of certain values, we take risks because we want to do certain things. We don't create energy for the sake of creating energy; we create energy because we want to do certain things with energy. So oddly enough it's impossible to calculate the acceptability of risk, at least as I saw it in the seminar that I ran, because all the calculations of the statistician and the engineer give us a component of a system which is not terribly important. The really important component is the value system in which you operate—what you want to do with the technological development, innovation, that you have in mind, so that in reality one cannot, in my opinion, think about the planning of technological society without trying to analyze the value system within which we operate and especially the kind of values that we want to create for the future. And as soon as you introduce those value problems, you discover that the term *acceptability of risk* becomes essentially meaningless, because we are so unclear as to the values that we want to cultivate and even more unclear as to the values that we want to leave to those who will follow us. And in my opinion this value system is what determines the extent to which we achieve happiness. And I'm going to contrast happiness with *joie de vivre*.

The *joie de vivre* is a purely biological experience, totally independent of what goes on. Happiness is highly conditioned by purely intellectual systems. You probably know that the etymology of the word *happiness* is to make something *happen.* I have tried to look in all sorts of dictionaries how one defines happiness, and there are two definitions in the unabridged Oxford dictionary. Both of them refer to the fact that happiness depends upon making something happen, and both indicate that there must be some kind of success in the enterprise that we undertake. The first definition of happiness is "good fortune or luck in a particular effort, success and prosperity in something that we undertake." Then the second is "the state of pleasurable content of mind which results from success or from the attainment of what is considered good." So all of a sudden you see the word *success.* The word *happiness* implies that we have elected to do something, that we want it to succeed, and we are happy when that happening results in the thing that we wanted to achieve. But that does not mean at all that happiness depends upon making our life more comfortable, giving us pleasures of the flesh, or even entertaining us. As you all know, many people find happiness in electing to do things that may be painful, that may be highly demanding, that may even involve sacrifice, self-sacrifice. We all know of people who are happy only, or chiefly, when they do something for others from which they do not realize any benefit for themselves.

There comes to my mind a phrase, an extraordinary statement, from the notebooks of Leonardo da Vinci, that I jotted down many years ago with several exclamation marks. It is in Italian, naturally: *Leonardo perché tanto peni?* "Leonardo, why do you give yourself so much trouble?"

Happiness for Leonardo meant those phenomenal efforts all of his life, to try to achieve something that did not bring him comfort, did not bring him money, did not make him more important, but that he considered worthwhile. I think the experience of happiness is something that probably is very peculiarly human, because it's so completely independent of the purely biological aspects of life. It all depends upon achieving something which transcends biological necessity. The first artifacts that we have of human life are those from the Old Stone Age in Europe. I shall mention only those phenomenal paintings in the Old Stone Age caves of Spain and especially of southern France. As you probably know, all those paintings are in the depths of caves, extremely uncomfortable, cold, wet, where the painter had to climb over rocks and engage in the most difficult physical tricks to be able to design animals and human beings under these conditions. One knows that the total population of Spain and of France at that time, thirty thousand years ago, was no more than fifty thousand people. Yet in Spain and France and other parts of Europe there are hundreds of such caves with those phenomenal paintings, and new ones are being discovered all the time. This must mean that a very large percentage of the total social effort was devoted to doing things which did not bring a crumb of bread or any kind of comfort to that prehistoric society.

Let us look at Stonehenge in England. Or, if you will, at the Carnac alignments in French Brittany, or the immense statues of Easter Island. Again, we know that the population at that time was extremely small—a few thousand people. We know that those immense stones had to be brought from very great distances. We know that erecting these phenomenal monuments of Stonehenge several thousand years ago was an extraordinary technological feat when there were very few people doing it, which means that the society must have devoted an enormous percentage of its human and technical resources, and of its time, to creating things that certainly did not help the purely biological aspects of life.

I could go on and on. Just think of the number of cathedrals that were built at the end of the twelfth century and the very beginning of the thirteenth century. And if I speak of the French cathedrals around Paris, it's simply because I happen to have been born and raised in that part of the world, and I know a great many details. Each of the cathedral towns had only about ten thousand people. And yet every ten or twenty years a new cathedral was being built. I know the history of all of them. And interestingly enough, each cathedral was a little higher than the last—higher by about twenty feet. One knows exactly the measurements. Practically the whole society was involved in the creation of these buildings. You may say, well, that was because of religious inspiration, and I assume that this played a role in it. But I know it was not only that, because, as historical documents reveal, there is no doubt that each little town wanted to do something a little bigger than the last one. So that each cathedral was about twenty feet higher than the one built ten years before in the city with which the other city wanted to compete. Obviously, the necessity to build something spectacular as a collective enterprise was still very strong at that time. It was obviously still very strong in Italy during the early Renaissance when Siena was a very small city— perhaps five or six thousand people—and yet constructed those phenomenal buildings which make us ashamed that we have not been able to complete, after a hundred years, the cathedral of St. John the Divine in New York City.

You may say these collective enterprises which do not aim at achieving biological comfort are something of the past and no longer for our time, but, as a matter of fact, I suspect that these are precisely the things that we are still most proud of. The great event of our time, from the point of view of a collective enterprise, was unquestionably the landing on the moon. It was a phenomenal achievement in which a whole community in some way or another did engage, because somebody voiced it as a worthwhile goal for society. I think we can also see some of this in Israel. I have had occasion to discuss many times the creation of the early kibbutz in Israel, some thirty years ago, and I had the good fortune to visit some. It's obvious that the creation of the kibbutz was not just an attempt to create a place to live, because it's much easier to live in Haifa or Tel Aviv or Jerusalem. It certainly had a meaning that transcended practicing agriculture on the land. It was creating a new way of life. Even today, as you probably know, though Israel has become a highly industrialized country, about 4 percent of the population still elect to live in a kibbutz. And it is still a very difficult life.

Out of all this, I have formed a very tentative conclusion—that happiness depends upon our willingness to engage in some activity that transcends biological necessities. And preferably to engage in some activity that has a meaning for the collectivity, for the community, and, even better, a meaning for the future. This is a highly intellectual process, one that cannot be defined in biological terms, and one which, I believe, is peculiar to human life.

Returning to technology, I think the great problem of our time will be to make technology conform to human nature, to physical nature and to human aspirations, instead of our accepting to conform to technology as has been the case until about 1940 or 1950. This may help us to see where technology can help us. I believe that technology can help us in what I call *joie de vivre* by creating environments in which we can give a more complete expression to our biological attributes. *Joie de vivre* depends upon our biological perception of the environment. Certainly technology can make that more difficult, but if it were used more intelligently, it could also make *joie de vivre* much richer. Then technology can certainly enhance what I have called happiness, because it enlarges so much the range of our enterprises, and especially it's beginning to help us perceive the consequences for the future of the activities we engage in today. I believe this is a very new aspect of modern life, that for the first time, during the past twenty years, we have begun through technological manipulation to be able to anticipate the long-range future consequences of what we undertake. And because we have begun to anticipate the long-range consequences, we naturally have this kind of uneasiness about what we are doing today. But this uneasiness is one of the most wonderful attributes of human beings, because it illustrates that we are worried not so much for ourselves because in reality we are not suffering much from technology. We are chiefly worrying about what it might mean for the future, for people whom we do not know, for people whose life we cannot imagine, what it might mean if we are not wise enough to create a technology which is safe for the natural world and which also permits human aspirations to continue developing and continue the social evolution of humankind.

QUESTION: How can we find a principle which will enable us to make technological discoveries which will not change, result in a reversal of their original aim? We make a discovery which we think will relieve us of something, and twenty years later we discover it's killing us. What sort of principle can we find which can obviate this risk? I look at Chinese medicine—I studied acupuncture—and I see that three or four thousand years ago certain principles were laid down, and today they are still true.

DUBOS: First of all let me bring you up to date on acupuncture. Some three or four years ago it was shown that there is a whole new class of hormones in the brain called endorphins, which are very similar in their action to heroin, morphine, and other opiates. Very similar; in fact, identical. It was demonstrated recently that by acupuncture manipulation you can increase the secretion of these hormones, which in turn decrease the perception of pain.

Now, as to what we can do about preventing a technological development which is useful when it is first introduced from becoming a threat later, well, let me first give examples from medicine, then move to other technological examples. When I began in medical research more than fifty-one years ago, anyone that developed anything that appeared useful could put it on the market and sell it, and it was used. But now no new drug can be put on the market unless it is subjected to a whole battery of tests with regard to the effects of that substance on human beings. Moreover, even those tests have changed in character during the past four or five years. At first, when this safety control was introduced, one looked for acute effects. One would, for example, inject a large amount of a given drug or a hormone or a new substance into an animal and see whether that substance had acute toxic effects. The law now requires tests to measure the very long-range effect on the whole lifetime of an animal. And the science which is only now beginning to develop is very difficult to manage, because we have begun to insist on this kind of projection into the future of the consequences of the innovations that we introduce.

The same thing is happening in technology, of course, only on an even larger scale. As you know, during the past few years the laws of environmental impact have been passed. Any innovation must be accompanied by a statement, a study, which is called a statement of environmental impact, in which one has to try to anticipate the effect of the technical innovation on the total environment, not only for the immediate here and now, but also into the future.

So the question of obviating the risks in introducing new techniques has become almost an obsession within our society. We still don't know very well how to do it, but unquestionably within the past twenty years much progress has been made toward making sure that we do not do what we've done in the past, namely, introduce technologies that later prove to be dangerous.

QUESTION: What do you think will happen to the *joie de vivre?* I have felt it once in a while in myself, and I see it in young children, but it isn't something I see much among adults, nor is it something that lasts a long time.

DUBOS: This is perhaps the most important question of modern times. No, I am not saying that to flatter you. I ask myself the same question all the time and will give you some of the answers I find within myself. *Joie de vivre* implies the ability to apprehend the *whole* of creation around you. And of course, as you say, children have that. Then, as we grow up, through mishandled processes of socialization, as I see it, we atrophy. We interfere with and mask our ability to perceive the environment and to perceive the quality of the cosmos. I believe there are people who retain it to the end of their lives. I believe I have. And I cultivate it. I make sure, to the extent that it is possible, that everytime I have to do something, I do it in such a way that I perceive the total situation in which I am. I like to watch you smile when I say that. When I go to my dentist in New York City, I arrange to take time to walk so as to see the immense diversity of people in the street. The experience of going to the dentist is supplemented by the phenomenal richness of these impressions. And, since I believe this is the most important question of our time, I have tried to see whether it has been stated in literature in some way that would summarize the meaning of your question. It happens that one of the greatest poets of the late nineteenth century wrote a marvelous phrase, which is in French, and I'm going to translate it. The name of the poet is Baudelaire, in case you want to know. *Le génie, c'est l'enfance retrouvée.* Genius is childhood recaptured. And each one of us retains to the end of our life the potential for that *joie de vivre,* but somehow or other we overload our life with things that prevent us from continuing to give expression to it. By the way, if you want to sense how long it can persist, I remember a few years ago seeing some of the primitive people of Australia and seeing the phenomenal joy that persists among the adults and the old people.

Very recently, Professor Alexander Leaf, the Chairman of the Department of Medicine at Harvard University, undertook a study of very old people in different parts of the world—in Central America, in Turkestan, as I recall, and southern Russia—and brought out a book about that. I can't remember the title of the book. It shows pictures of people in their eighties, nineties, and so on, and all those people have created a society in which they continue to be active to the end of their life. Whereas the folly of our society is to think that, once you have made enough money to be comfortable, you should sit in your chair and watch a spectacle and no longer participate with your own body in life. *Joie de vivre* depends upon your opportunity to participate in everything that happens around you.

QUESTION: If I understand you, you were talking today about the cathedrals in Asia, in India, in France, and Stonehenge, as examples of common work of humans toward a common goal. I am confused about that, because, on the one hand, as humans right now we seem to treat these things with an enormous wonder, but we also seem to have a compulsion to understand them. We see all these books, *Stonehenge Decoded* and so on, and there are books in a sense about the decoding of say, a painting. I wonder if you care to comment on these two aspects of art appreciation?

DUBOS: About Stonehenge, about even the early cathedrals, it's obvious that people did not try to understand these. They perceived them with their *whole* beings. Now I just think they did not *try* to understand; they had simply to look. Some documents from the Stone Age have been discovered that indicate they were more intellectual than we had assumed till now. I would like to tell you a story even though it's somewhat removed from your question. During the Apollo Moon Program, NASA hired a person named Alexander Marshak to publicize the Apollo program. To this end he familiarized himself with all aspects of lunar science, in particular with lunar cycles. Then one day he found in *Scientific American* a picture of an ivory blade from the Stone Age.

This blade had large numbers of scratchings so spaced that he guessed they might represent moon cycles. He abandoned his NASA position and went to Europe, where he studied other Stone Age objects of bone and ivory to confirm his hypothesis. He has now become an expert on the thought processes of Stone Age people.

Peter Crossley-Holland

Peter Crossley-Holland *has worked throughout his life to open modern people to the role of music in the search for consciousness. Starting as a composer with an experimental interest in Pythagorean theory, he is now Professor of Music at UCLA. In a city where technology is "modernizing" music, he has attracted attention as an authority on the sacred music of Tibet and other parts of the East.*

MUSIC IS NOT an isolated phenomenon. It is everywhere a part of human life at many levels and is subject to the same forces, aspirations, and changes as other aspects of human culture. Today the main emphasis in musical life is clear: It is the machine—disc, tape, radio, and film—and, as we shall see, the most machinelike parts of man. In former times the emphasis was different. In the Renaissance it was not man and the machine, but man and man —music in human society. Still earlier, in the Middle Ages, it was different again: music and the word of God and man's relationship with God. Thus as concepts have changed from theocentric to anthropocentric and thence to technocentric, Western music over the last thousand years has shown a tremendous outward thrust. During the present century, and especially since the 1950s, the results have become painfully apparent, and I want to examine with you some critical aspects of our present situation.

To understand how musical life today has come about, it will be sufficient if we first go back, briefly, some two centuries. At that time, in the 1770s, European art still reflected a stable order of society. Fine music was heard in religious ritual; folk song helped to sustain the labors of the peasants and to enliven their leisure hours, while the music we now call classical provided a refined form of recreation in the social lives of the privileged class. Just two hundred years ago, for instance, in 1778, the middle-aged Haydn was composing works for Prince Esterhazy, and the young Mozart was on a stay in Paris completing his symphony of that name (No. 31 in D, K.102).

Mozart, Haydn, and many other composers were speaking in a common musical language that all could understand, and music was one of the very binding forces of European society. The so-called industrial revolution was in its childhood, and, if anything, the new developments looked like bringing prospects for better living.

If we now leap forward a century, musical life was already different. Composers had turned away from the old order of society—there was already much that was degenerate about the aristocracy—and, reacting against the ugliness created by more than a hundred years of industry, not to mention the untutored and sentimental standards of the bourgeoisie, they were gradually retreating into worlds of their own imagination. Just one hundred years ago, in 1878, Grieg composed his *Album Leaves* for piano and the thirty-eight-year-old Tchaikowsky was hearing the first performance of his *Symphony No. 4* in Moscow.

The music we refer to as romantic was increasingly concerned with "destiny" and the cult of the individual, and it gradually led away from tradition and a common language toward personal tongues not hitherto so generally accessible. Later this led to extremes of musical speech, so that what at first looked like a refuge from commerce somehow partook of the very sense of individualism generated by capitalist society, and it began to head for the ivory tower.

By that same year, 1878, the old world had only just begun to hear of some very new inventions in the United States: Edison's phonograph of 1877 and Bell's microphone of 1876, and Muybridge's experiments in the same decade which later led to the motion picture (1899), parent of the sound film (1927). It was to be some time before Marconi's experiments in the 1890s brought radio into general use (1919). But at the end of the nineteenth century, no one knew how musical life throughout the whole world would be totally changed through the three new media—recording, radiotransmission, and film.

If we leap forward again, another hundred years to 1978, we find ourselves in an entirely changed world, with the first purely synthetic music in history, music programmed directly by its composer into a digital computer. An example of this is a piece by Vladimir Ussachevsky, one of the pioneers of electronic music in this country, called *Computer Piece No. 1.*

Along with this rather *recherché* type of music, a great flood of music of more familiar types is being constantly poured out through record and radio today, and, for most people, this is the only music they ever hear. For those actively pursuing some line of musical development or education, the media offer unprecedented opportunities. But one important question that arises concerns what we are paying for these advantages. Educators have often urged that the constantly sounding radio has great potential for the education of the masses, but they failed to anticipate the actual results. Since the public, upon whom all kinds of music has been indiscriminatley released, has in the main been ill prepared to receive it, the effect has been the opposite of that hoped for. The false sense of authority attached to the radio, placing equal emphasis upon everything, has left the masses confused.

All forms and styles are mixed into the ceaseless radio sound, and people are encouraged to believe that they have both the right and the ability to judge it all. Yet at best—and we have to be clear about this—radio listeners are consumers of canned goods, in a diet largely decided for them by others. And somewhere in the process of canning the essential flavor has been lost.

The situation is worse yet. Not only are we free to surround ourselves with music day and night, but also we *must* do so, for our neighbors' radios are all around. Radios and public-address systems are at work everywhere we go: in the factories; in the shops; in restaurants, airports, and airplanes; in our cars and local taxi and also in the dentist's chair; on sportsfields; in playgrounds; and, yes, even in the common rooms of university campuses, blaring out music in its least cultured manifestations. But that is not enough: people have to take their transistor sets into the streets, on the beaches, and far into the countryside and mountains to despoil nature of the elemental peace that some people still seek. As long ago as 1952 Max Picard wrote in his book *The World of Silence* that "man completely loses touch with the spontaneous element in life" and that he "has become merely an appendage of the sound of the radio."

We are, there is no doubt of it, suffering from *innundation by music*. This, then, is one of the prices we have paid. So I want to look rather carefully into the effects of the media on several aspects of music making. Since the case for the defense has been pleaded many times, I am going rather to put the case for the prosecution tonight. Certainly much of what I am going to say will strike you as unpalatable, yet we have to be possessed of certain essential facts before we can consider more promising approaches. So please bear with me awhile.

Let us look first at the role of music in human society. Until recently both musical contexts and musical forms were much determined by factors lying at the very roots of communal life—the calendar, the seasons, rites of passage, and all the variety of well-regulated social occasions, each involving its proper times, places, and persons. Music helped to articulate the life of society on all levels: work and recreation; beliefs and aspirations; communication by man with his fellows, with his inmost self and his gods. Such is the real meaning of what we call a music culture, that is, a circuit of music making in which almost everybody, however modestly, plays some part, and in which, above all, people *make* music.

As Wilfrid Mellers (*Music in the Making,* 1962) has argued, when educators speak of radio bringing great music to the masses, they are completely uncomprehending of what musical culture really is. In effect, a music culture based on the mass media can only be a pseudo-culture, rootless, formless, and homeless. The solid body of practicing amateurs, who were well-informed listeners and a continuing source of stimulation to the efforts of composers in the past, has disappeared today; the amateur with any musical literacy is rather rare. In his place we have the passive listener, who does not even know how much work it takes to establish any real contact with music. Perhaps it all began with the ease of turning a knob, but in any case there can be no active participation in listening to a machine. And thus it is that *people* are rapidly disappearing from music: gone are the social occasions, the associated sights and sounds, so that music, no longer rooted in the deeper structures of life, has to be considered mere "art for art's sake." This very expression challenges historical and anthropological evidence alike; namely, that the arts are largely oriented positively, toward man's search for a more secure and ordered existence.

It is true that the motion picture provides a definite context for music, but, with all the cutting and the relatively amorphous state of so many films as art forms, film fails to provide scope for musical forms on a par with those that were deeply linked with social contexts in the past. It must be admitted, too, that film music is rarely of much cultural value. And because of the glamor attaching to the screen, many peoples, not only of the West but also of the East, not to mention the North and the South, once happy with their music in traditional styles, are now pathetically striving to imitate their posturing screen idols.

Most of the music heard today in the Western world falls into three very broad classes: popular, serious and ethnic, and each class has, in the main, its own listeners.

The music of the masses is commercially inspired popular music, which also includes the calculated nonmusic known as Muzak. When I was asked to visit a well-known American university about ten years ago, I found that large numbers of my students sat with their radios on for hours on end, listening—or more often probably not listening—to what their commercial stations decided they should listen to; and, as they confessed, how very few of them had ever attended an actual concert of music in their lives! The commercial music they heard, which they often referred to as folk music, was of course not folk music at all. Commercials have replaced the old folk music by an imposed music allowing no scope for creative participation and, having no individual or local personality but an ill-defined global one, serving to link a world that is mutually dependent commercially but in no other way. You know the kind of thing I mean: songs whose subject matter reflects the same sham emotion as does commercial advertising, when, that is, they are not simply parodies on other musical styles. Designed to keep the attention on the sensuous surface, this music, which rates sensation and even immediate gratification above order, appeals to the most machinelike parts of man and keeps him on the periphery of experience. Jazz masses are little better; their very obviously physical type of movement puts the emphasis in an inappropriate place. Intellectually, the words of the songs occasionally rise to a sort of pseudo-philosophy, but they are then at their most dangerous, and the captive young audience is at its most vulnerable.

The most insidious thing about commercial music is that, like the advertisements, it tries to sell you something you don't really want; it tries to sell you the idea that the periphery of life *is* life itself. And if you listen to lies about yourself over and over again, the likelihood is that you may come to believe them and to doubt your own identity. Now I am not saying that this music is not sometimes attractive or that it is not technically competent; it may be devastatingly so. But when you surround yourself with it continuously, the overstimulation can easily lead to a state of neurotic indecision. A promiscuous desire for nothing but entertainment is, in effect, on a par with drug addiction. There is, moreover, a business conspiracy to pander to it. Further, just as sensations, when they are allowed to stray away from the whole of man, quickly pall, so also does the music; it rapidly goes out of fashion and there is a constant demand for something "new." Yet, musically speaking, commercials are hardly even definable in contemporary terms; they owe so much to the commonplaces of serious music in the not-so-recent past, made trite by being taken out of their proper settings. And what an outcry if anyone dares voice the slightest doubts about our allegedly perfect situation!

The listener who wants to find something deeper and more lasting in music, the "serious" listener, is also in a debatable position. He usually chooses to live chiefly in the past, listening to the music of the eighteenth and nineteenth centuries. It seems unnatural that, for the great majority of serious listeners, older music should form their exclusive diet. This has never happened in the past. There is also the interesting question as to how it is that the music to which most of us still turn for our most significant models was created directly for a form of society found unacceptable today? This cannot be answered so easily, yet today people seem to turn to the older music as a refuge from the conflicts of life; so this, too, may be considered a reaction against the problems created by the spread of technology. At the same time, it may be noted that the art of truly great composers of the past has, as it were, radiated well beyond its own time. Placing order above sensation, great music has ever sought a new balance in relation to man's complex makeup. Very varied in its range of human experience, it has, at its best, been concerned with spiritual values. The fact that we can respond to the higher in music suggests that we already have this higher in ourselves, even though it be often overlaid. Indeed, great music, like lesser music, can also tell us "this is what you really are," and it can tell us so with greater truth.

All the same, when this music is heard on radio or disc, the familiar objections stand. Though he may derive some stimulus for his own music making, the listener does not actively participate.

If the conservative musical listener lives chiefly in the past, quite otherwise is it with those very few who go along with the music of the so-called avant-garde. For many composers have made a deliberate break with the past and have studiedly avoided anything that seems to refer to the past. I should explain that much of this music, whose immediate roots lie in the 1950s, has already reached the ivory tower. Already at the turn of the century romanticism was giving way to individualism and idiosyncrasy (with their self-centered worlds of make-believe) and then to impressionism (with its emphasis on the sensations of the moment), and music has since traveled much further. Meanwhile, alongside these developments, the actual materials of music were beginning to change. By the turn of the century, also, many composers no longer accepted the traditional hierarchy of pitches, so that tonality was giving way to atonality and polytonality—developments thought to have started around 1890–1910 with the American composer Charles Ives. By 1921–1923 the Austrians Hauer and Schoenberg had developed systems of composing with all twelve notes of the chromatic octave. With Schoenberg these were repeated in every phrase; the twelve notes were now considered arbitrarily equal in their own right, and the result was tonal anarchy. Whereas Hauer's system, whose metaphysical underlay derived inspiration from Goethe, hardly saw the light of day, the method of the more assertive Schoenberg has had a tremendous vogue over a large part of the world. But his own music turns out to be more or less "private" and, in sober retrospect, to have no general social validity. It is of interest that the emotional content of serial music in general offers little food for the heart; the feelings are so often those of violence and self-pity, and, like the heroes of this music, they are typically psychopathological.

Other composers championed new forms of classicism for a time, but from World War II onward serialism became the principal stream. It was not long, indeed, before serial techniques became extended to all ultimate elements of sound, that is, to duration, amplitude, and tone quality as well as to pitch. Music shortly became totally predetermined in its form. It was around this time, the early 1950s, moreover, that electronic sound was substituted for that of real instruments and that, for the first time in world history, music became synthetic. One consequence of these developments was that an attempt was made to eliminate human emotion and to focus on mechanism in music, though in practice the music has often exploited sensation in its most barbaric forms. Representing, too, as its composers aver, a deliberate and radical break with the past, and having for the average man no clear point of contact with the present, it must seem to him like some music of the future; its "science fiction" atmosphere suggests as much, and the music seems most at home when accompanying science fiction films and films based on scientific approaches to ESP. Yet this future must be an imaginary one, for in so many ways the music does not correspond to human modes either of expression or of perception and fails to communicate on any levels other than those of immediate sensation or purely mental abstraction. Using limited areas of the composer's makeup, it can only be the result of fragmented being, and such is what the average well-educated listener surely feels. I shall have more to say about this music when we come to consider the effects of the media on the composer and creativity.

A third group of listeners has become significant since the war, through new contacts of the West with the Eastern world. Tours of Asian musicians, at first especially musicians from India, drew attention to remarkable forms of music making whose roots lie deeper in human history than our own. Much of this music is more intuitively based than ours, whereas rational considerations, forever on the increase with us, are little more than peripheral. Although musical contacts between great cultures have existed in the past and have borne fruit, history tells us that they have been on a more limited scale (China-Japan; Persia-India). The sudden global confrontation precipitated by the media has posed many problems for forms of music so different in their concepts, natures, and needs.

In the first place, the Oriental music has, like our own, been taken out of context and made to join the faceless flow of radio sound. Musicians playing high art forms were presented alongside rock groups; facile and false comparisons were made, values were wantonly confused, and the music was separated from its traditional approaches to listening, without which it could convey only a superficial and even misleading impression of what, given the proper time, place, and circumstance, could seem miraculous.

Then there was the whole question of what the global contacts would do for the forms and techniques of Oriental music. International conferences of musicians and scholars met during the 1960s in various cities of the East and West, hoping to find ways of offsetting the widespread confusion created by haphazard contacts throughout the globe. UNESCO, the International Folk Music Council, and other bodies played a part, and some useful countercurrents were set up. Recommendations made were designed to deepen the sense of responsibility: of radios, as to what they might put out; of educators, as to the perspectives in which music might be taught; and of government bodies, in respect to their duties regarding native musical heritage. Our hope was that the "preservation" and selective dissemination of music, as well as creative and scholarly exchange, would help to renew the older traditions. But theoretical programs of this sort are always apt to reckon without three essential things: first, that renewal of music depends upon renewal of society; second, that it calls for genius; and third, that neither of these is at our direct disposal.

Meanwhile, the commercial boys were busy exploiting recordings of Oriental and African music, seizing upon every superficially attractive feature, dressing it up in their ephemeral popular pieces designed to keep their listeners just where *they* wanted them. Thus for many listeners discovery of the real Oriental music is already spoiled.

The various groups of listeners we have considered—popular, serious, and ethnic—represent only parts of the whole, albeit important parts. There are also those interested in new music in more approachable forms, the devotees of the Middle Ages and the Renaissance, those who prefer jazz, and so on. As a matter of fact, we have more "musics" today than we ever had before. Yet, strangely, we have no single music that we can truly call our own. Why?

Now we leave the listener and turn to the performer. Over the media, the listener has no exchange with the performer; there is no give and take. True of the West, this is even more noticeable in the East, as in Indian *raga* music, for instance, where the momentary exchange may go into the very make of the music itself. But everywhere the radio performer enters the padded studio alone, without expectancy or human murmur, and faces a cold silence at the end. And sponsored radio announcers, also part of the performance, so often start speaking immediately after the sound has ceased, unaware, it seems, that much music ends appreciably after the final sound has been heard. Clearly, they are afraid: But is their fear of the silence or, perhaps, of losing a few cents?

One of the ways in which the media have affected performance is in the matter of technique, for recorded music is intended for repeat, and even minute errors, which may go for nothing in the concert hall, cannot be perpetuated on a disc. So recording favors performers of a certain class, and the public may never come to know of other types. In the earlier days of the media the situation called for sensitive artists who were also good technicians, but now technique often becomes an end in itself. Overstress on virtuosity is included by the great sociologist Pitrim Sorokin (*Social and Cultural Dynamics,* 1937) among the characteristics typical of sensate art, that is, of art based on the belief that only what our senses tell us can be true. There is, too, the question of patchwork recording, where, should the performer make a mistake or want to play a passage with greater virtuosity, he rerecords that part and has it incorporated by means of tape splicing. The result, though it may sound "perfect," has no organic unity, does not correspond to any one actual experience, has an element of make-believe. Virtuosity begets nothing but virtuosity. The cults of technique and virtuosity stress mechanism at the expense of spirit. And since such music can address itself only to the machine in man, no wonder he feels that something is lacking.

This brings us to the quality of the media themselves. Whereas the media work largely in terms of stereotyped time periods, music is not so conceived. The disc began life in 1896 by recording a very few minutes per side, and even the incidence of electric recording in 1925 did not alter that. It was not until 1948 that the advent of the so-called long-playing disc increased the side to a maximum of twenty-five minutes or so—still not long enough to avoid musical surgery—though discovery of magnetic tape in 1950 has much helped.

On broadcast programs time is similarly cut up, though for other reasons. On sponsored radio, complete works are very rarely heard. Music is interrupted by inept advertisements with their own finicky music of a different kind. Sometimes fragments from great works, taken out of their true setting, are mixed with brash salesmanship and so are made to acquire associations altogether foreign to their nature. Even radio free of such fuss typically operates in stereotyped periods, though I recall a glorious era on the Third Programme of the BBC., where the periods were timed to fit the music and not vice versa. This must be exceptionally rare.

By reason of this type of limitation larger pieces are actually disappearing in the Eastern world. In the case of Indian classical music, where a single performance ideally needs an hour at the very least, evoking and sustaining as it does a particular emotional state, the time segmentation of radio and gramophone performances makes the music to be less than it actually is. Again, the end of a performance is not determined by what may be natural to a given occasion where there is a constant exchange between people, but by the need to conform to a purely mechanical time limit. And the popular call for variety within a program further aggravates the position. As a result music dependent upon improvisation is less frequently heard in some countries.

There is also the quality of sound. Despite much vaunted labels like "Hi Fi," reproduced sound only approximates the original; even at its impressive best, it still remains canned. Unfortunately, however, sound is not always well canned. Forms of stereophonic recording have helped since the 1950s (tape 1955, disc 1958), but much of what passes for "stereo" is artificially added, sometimes with ludicrous results. And why? because companies are afraid that their discs will otherwise fail to sell; so they are happy to sell make-believe. Again, discs can wear out pretty quickly; they can also crack, and I know a well-known music station in California where I have heard the same cracked performances several times.

When frequency modulation came in before World War II, it extended the upper range of transmission to 15,000 cps. or so, though due to imperfections in the transmission chain (microphone, amplifier, transmitter, receiver) the ceiling rarely exceeds 10,000 cycles even today. Thus many higher frequencies existing in the tone quality of the music are not actually heard, and the bloom of the sound is lost. Speaking of which, the hearing organs of many habitués of loud rock music have been found to be like those of persons aged sixty-five, and that before they are even out of their teens. Sad to tell, the finer sounds will never again exist for them. So what if they be composers?

Then there is the matter of reception. First, the quality of reception is naturally limited by the equipment that people can afford. There may also be interference from other wavelengths and unfavorable atmospheric conditions, and receivers set at so high a level as to distort. Again, as I need hardly say, radio music heard at home is rarely free from interruption, whether by telephone, by callers, or by members of the family.

Though people are rarely directly aware of it, halls and classrooms where music is taught often have two continuous sounds of their own, arising from the lighting and air-conditioning plants. Such sounds undoubtedly interfere with the music at a subtle (and sometimes not so subtle) level. I remember being laughed at when I dared to mention this in an American university where I have taught, even though my opinion was invited as to conditions considered ideal for a new music building. It is astonishing to find such complacency among those who might be expected to be sensitive to these things.

All these problems really concern efficiency. For if there is one thing that is required of a machine, it is that *it should be efficient.* But the listener's experience is very rarely so. No wonder his own inner machine feels uncomfortable! And as for the way that music is retailed over public-address systems, with their cheap microphones and their irresponsibly high volume, it is hardly surprising if he feels positively upset.

The developments in musical instruments during the twentieth century have stemmed largely from two causes: mass audiences and mass media, that is, essentially from considerations of quantity. It is not only a question of instruments being mass produced or made with new and synthetic materials. Where a mass audience is present, as in a large hall, so-called improved instruments are used; this applies, for instance, to many Oriental examples, where silk strings have been replaced by wire, which gives a greater volume of sound; but this also calls for different playing techniques, and so it already becomes a *different* sound. Another way in which a louder sound may be obtained is, of course, through electrical amplification. If certain stringed instruments of the East (e.g., Indian *sitar,* Chinese *ch'in*) are used in large halls without some amplification, many essential nuances may be lost. Amplification, however, so often introduces distortion.

At the same time, reproduction of instruments over the media has given rise to some new "ideals" of sound, ranging from clinical clarity to echo effects.

All in all, therefore, instrument builders were long ago beginning to respond to the general rise in sound level of our time as well as to the possibilities of the new media. Since amplification could best be done by electrical means, the idea arose of building in the electric medium as an actual part of the instrument itself. The sound, still activated by the player, is converted into electric waves and amplified (sometimes modified too), and then the waves are reconverted into sound by means of an inbuilt loudspeaker. The best known example of this type of instrument is the electric guitar, used extensively in popular music. In this way a relatively small instrument can be made to give a large volume of sound, with obvious economic advantages. But the question stands: Will the beauty of natural instruments ever be surpassed by electrical means?

More recent instrument types have dispensed with natural sounds altogether and have replaced them with synthetic sounds. The "new" sounds originate directly in electric tone generators. At this point the instrument has finally broken with all natural sounds. Though experimental forms actually go back to the turn of the century, it is in the 1920s that they begin to come into musical use. One of these, called the *ondes Martenot* (*ondes musicales,* musical waves), was used by Honegger in his oratorio *Joan of Arc at the Stake* (1935). Honegger was first among the composers of his generation to lament the mechanistic tendencies of modern life, and he reacted against them in some of his choral works. It is significant that he uses the *ondes* not all the time but in well-calculated passages where it heightens the sense of tragedy.

Perhaps the best known of all instruments in this class is the Hammond organ, though here I want to point out a feature not present in the other instruments. The partials (or inner notes of any given sound) do not exactly follow the harmonic series; in the interests of economy in construction, they are tempered; that is to say, they compromise with a particular law of sound. Now while it is true that, although musical sound has a reference frame in mathematical proportions, it only departs from this within *organic* limits, in the Hammond organ the departure occasioned by tempering the partials is itself *mathematical* and, to that extent, goes against the musical process. The difference between tempered and real partials is not so great as to be immediately perceptible to the average ear, but the question remains as to what this compromise is doing to the human organism. What is happening to the molecules?

It was somehow inevitable that musical instruments would soon develop beyond this point. In the 1950s, when so many "new" things were happening in music, a still newer type of instrument evolved: the electronic instrument making electronic music. By means of the synthesizer or the digital computer, a composer who has some knowledge of electronic engineering can create music directly by doing three things simultaneously: by generating the sounds of his composition on such a machine, by transforming them in a variety of ways, and by recording them on magnetic tape. This method makes a score unnecessary and actually eliminates the performer altogether. It thus represents a further step in the dehumanization of music. As well as doing away with "imperfections" in performance, the electronic instruments eschew all the subjective feelings a performer might convey. In effect, the performer and the composer are now one. His instrument can go far beyond what an ordinary instrument can realize in terms of pitch range, complexity of texture, nuance of tone quality, extremes of loudness, and so on. The sounds are naturally at home on tape and, by the same token, seem completely out of place in a concert hall. In such music each work only and ever has a single performance. That performance is not conceived for "now" but is fixed for "ever," even though the acoustic environment and the audience may change.

As I said earlier, electronic music was first evolved in the 1950s. At its origin it converged with advanced serialism, thus achieving a marriage of total formal predetermination with laboratory sound. Leading composers involved were Karlheinz Stockhausen in Germany and Milton Babbitt in the United States. At first, electronic music imitated known instruments, and the resulting impression was essentially ersatz. Rather significantly, the voice was eliminated. Later, it began to experiment with a "new" world of sounds, all synthetically produced.

The electronic composer's tone material is, in fact, generated in two complementary ways: namely, by the synthesis of sine tones and the analysis of "white noise." Such sounds, once generated, are subjected to all kinds of alteration in terms of *time* (by reversal, altered speed, expansion, and contraction); *pitch* (by extension of range, transposition, and nuance); and *tone* (by echo and by manipulation of the spectrum through reversal, filtering, and folding).

The essential question is, what does electronic music convey? A distinguished engineer who helped work out its principles in the electronic studio at Cologne Radio has confessed that "sounds generated by these means are often not sufficiently adapted to the

84

power of human perception and thus are not understood by the wide public" (Fritz Winckel, *Music, Sound and Sensation,* 1967). Looked at from the social perspective, electronic music, having broken with the past and also with significant human experience in the present, seems strangely without bearings. It is not written for any amateur body or with any lay music lover in mind; and it has no personal, regional, or national colors. Moreover, the style is already full of clichés. Many of its composers seem little interested in the actual sound, and by their own confession do not think in terms of human communication or emotion, only in terms of experiment, though to what *artistic* end this experiment may be directed is not explicitly stated. Many composers work along the lines of mathematical series, but since even these series are stated to be random, how can we even speak of an art any longer? And who is to know that some so-called composers are not really engineers in disguise?

What we normally think of as a gestalt, forming the creative intersection of all elements in a music culture, exists no more. The placing of exclusive trust in the rational, in technique, in quantity, and in mechanism, is working against art; for all art, albeit in very varying degree, is a product of the rational and the intuitive. Electronic music, says H. J. Kollreuter, "seems to proclaim the triumph of matter over spirit" (*Three Lectures on Music,* 1968). This is not to say that it is necessarily all this way. There are some signs that meaning is coming through. Also, at least, the electronic experiments have borne some fruit in related fields: They have helped to throw light on the aesthetic role of "noise" in music and have afforded us a deeper insight into the spectral ranges of musical instruments.

If we look for a philosophy behind electronic music, we find it not very articulate. The original idea was to achieve unity of musical thought and musical material, with the sounds themselves generating the structure of the musical composition. It was, more-over, supposed to be a music about the heightened perception of sound. But there is little consistency in the basic principles, and these tend to vary from work to work. The gimmicky titles often found may elicit a wry smile, but the tongue-in-cheek notes accompanying recordings are not very helpful to those who may want to understand.

The creators of this "ivory tower" music are, of all composers, the most vocal about the exclusivity of their approach. It is parallel to atomic research, they say, and audiences are too lazy to understand anything new. And the critics encourage them. But I would put my faith in the honesty of a cultivated audience rather than in the average critic. The fact is that cultivated audiences have rejected this music. One of the most specious claims put forward by its self-congratulatory coteries is on behalf of the music's modernity. Two eminent composers of our time have had something to say about this. Stravinsky wrote "we call anything modern that caters to our snobbishness" (*The Poetics of Music*, 1947); and Hindemith saw the proclamation of modernity as being used to cover up a poor technique (*A Composer's World*, 1953). In any case, the symptoms of modernity are linked with the compulsive search for novelty and with the insistence on so-called originality. A work has to be controversial in order to attract notice. But even a moment's reflection will show that a work of art can never be great *because* of its modernity, though it is possible that it might be so *despite* it. It is significant, I think, that the composers of history whom time has adjudged great were rarely if ever radical innovators, but those who, with singular genius, managed to articulate the essentials of their period. Every accelerated change in music can only create confusion for the listener, and it is certainly a sign of general instability. The equation "change equals progress" is demonstrably false. Critics have not only failed to grasp this but have further signally declined to project music's ethical character or to consider its deeper values.

Of course, some composers have themselves reacted against the mechanistic sense of direction so prevalent in our time. The most radical reaction was perhaps the so-called aleatory, or chance, music, which leaves the assembly or juxtaposition of composed materials to the performer. There have also been attempts to mix natural with synthetic sounds, to reinstate the voice, to return to natural sounds altogether, to experiment with quadraphonic sound, and all the rest. But, strangely, the essence of the situation changes not at all: whether it be a question of reaction against the machine or of the further use of it, the center remains the machine, the ultimate fetish of our age. Some composers feel that everything has now been tried, that there are not and cannot be any fresh materials, and that, for all their frenzied search for the "new," they are stranded in a state of restless stagnation. According to the great historian Arnold Toynbee, a failure of creative power in the creative minority is one of the major signs of a breakdown in civilization. And it is clear that acceleration in technology and in the belief in it can only end one way, namely, in technocracy; and that is about where we stand now.

So we come, at length, to the great questions: Can anything be done? Is there perhaps something we have overlooked? Or have we come at last to the point of no return?

From this point I want rather to change key, to leave generalities, and to begin sharing with you some ways in which I have tried to live with our situation myself. I want to look at matters more especially as a composer who became maturely creative from the 1950s. So I will not apologize, since these are the only things I can speak of with any certainty at all.

Like every young composer, I had to find answers to the questions: What is music? and Where am I going?

Ever since I can remember, I felt that music could open the door to a fuller life, a life where things happened in proper order. At first I felt this in the great classical music on which I was nurtured. But with youthful ardor I wanted to go beyond its uttermost bounds, to be one with God, love, and nature, and to capture this at-one-ment in sound. Many influences came to play their part. For instance, I steeped myself in the traditional music of the Celtic peoples, with whose mystery and beauty I felt a deep affinity. I received a new stimulus from listening to and playing mediaeval music, and I tried to penetrate the secrets of the Gothic cathedral composers, the troubadours, and the Christian saints. Each of these traditions had evidently tried to build a bridge to that other life I sought. I heard Indian and Chinese music in London, and later, when I managed to locate the recording of a single fragment of Tibetan ritual, I knew that I had found a music of unique power.

Alongside my love for the music itself, I became inquisitive about the principles hidden behind it. Through reading great myths about music in the Orient, I felt an echo of the music said to have miraculous powers, music which mortals might ever more nearly imitate but could never surpass. Some other studies I was making at the time led me to look into the connection of music with Christian symbolism; with freemasonry, alchemy, and astrology; and to seek references in all kinds of theosophical, mystical, and magical works. I wanted too much too quickly and gradually came to understand that this was not the way of it.

Nonetheless, all these things helped to awaken and sustain in me a sense of vision and to keep me close to the idea of that other order of life which I had already glimpsed. But how to enshrine this vision in music? How to express what so far remained unexpressed? How to clothe the formless in a form capable of reawakening the self-same presentiments? These were the questions which stayed with me. And they converged in a further very practical one: What musical materials should I use and with what techniques ought I to handle them?

In the first place, I should say that, despite the strong attraction much Oriental music held for me, my idea was to remain true to my own culture in musical terms. Yet, studying cross-cultural affinities of musical principle as well as inescapable differences, I wanted to find a means of creatively assimilating what I had learned, but at a subtle level where it would not stand out as something obviously coming from another tradition. In the search for materials I naturally also considered contemporary Western trends. Though for a time I studied Schoenberg's method of composing with twelve notes, I finally rejected it on several grounds. It was technically very mechanistic and seemed generally spiritless in the results. I could not accept the idea of tonal anarchy, or nominal equality, or the elements of arbitrary choice, or the fact that the tempered tuning of the twelve notes —acceptable as an expedient in keyboard music, where the harmonic intentions of the composer remained clear—was made to become a central pillar of this nonharmonic system, thus replacing natural with purely man-made law.

As time went on, I thought also about the possibilities of electrically generated sound. Neither the content nor the technique of the electronic music I had heard attracted me, either in its theatricality or in its highly cerebral approach, and I never felt at any time that I had to use the tools of a new technology creatively just because they were there. At the same time, electrical synthesis seemed to promise possibilities for exploring and studying pitch nuances and partials (the subtler sounds within a sound). With a friend I even drew up, in 1956, a preliminary specification for an organ which would enable us to experiment with pitch and spectral relationships, following guiding principles which would guard against both arbitrary selection and acoustic compromise. Our results were to be brought back into music making in more normal forms. But for various reasons that I need not relate this instrument never materialized.

So, in general, for musical material I still fell back upon the more distant past, with subtle inflections from Celtic music and from several Eastern traditions. Being of rather modest creative talent, I perhaps took more from such sources than more gifted composers have done. At the same time, I had a deep sense of connection with the stream of history. It was inevitable, therefore, that many of the works which bear my name should go back to an intuitive reenactment of ancient scenes.

On the more technical side I looked for organizing principles which, it seemed to me, ought to be valid not only in music but also in wider domains, so that, from the start, the music would serve as a window on larger perspectives. There were, therefore, very specifically the questions of how to proceed in matters of melody, rhythm, and form.

As regards form, I tried to link cyclic processes in music with cyclic processes in nature—so that time would, as it were, be shown as revolving around a more ultimate center. The canon or round in music could very well reflect natural recurrence. Thus in 1954, after studying all the rounds I could lay hands on, I wrote the words and music of *Two Dozen Rounds of Nature*. The words of one of them go like this:

> Round the earth the moon is moving,
> Round the sun the planets are turning,
> Round His throne they dance and sing.

Another idea was the growth of new forms out of age-old ones, for I felt that new branches and blossoms could always grow on an ancient trunk. One of the forms that interested me was the carol, an ancient type of song-dance which is properly defined not by its subject matter but by its form: choral burden, solo stanza, choral burden in continued alternation. I used this form in a cantata where Jesus Christ, in the style of a minstrel, recounts his life from his birth to his dwelling on the right hand of God. Each successive stanza is separated from the next by a choral burden or refrain, which ends with the words "This have I done for my true love." Following out this form, I expanded it further by separating off groups of stanzas (with their burdens) relating to different phases of Christ's life by means of orchestral interludes, which thus set the scene for new developments. This same work explores another idea too: that of different modes as elements in a musical language. As I am sure you know, in ancient Greece and in various different Oriental cultures, modes are associated with different ethical characters and associated moods. I studied this matter with a group of musical friends. Our idea was to work out anew the six melody modes of Western music, taking into full account their historical roots yet trying to link their structure with some larger ideas we were exploring at the time, and to see just how far they might be possessed of recognizably different ethical characters. In musical terms the results ranged from ultra-minor to ultra-major, and these extremes and their corresponding characters are, for instance, reflected in the contrast between the passages where Christ is tempted by the devil and betrayed by Judas on the one hand, and the uplifting sense of the recurrent burden on the other. The cantata is called *The Sacred Dance*.

These melody modes I also wanted to combine with rhythmic modes worked out on similar principles. I remember we mapped out six different rhythmic modes, which are, in effect, meters based on the various possible sequences of three note values of different lengths. Several of these rhythmic modes are embodied in a short *Meditation for Organ*. They are made to change constantly, suggesting the interplay of different modalities in nature and in man, yet they are all heard sounding above a drone or continuous unchanging pitch which, from my contact with Indian music, I always thought of not only as a tonic reference point in music but also as the Absolute reflected on the plane of sound. In this way the idea of change (the melodic and rhythmic modes) was heard against a background of the changeless (the drone). It may be of some interest that modern information theory maintains that a static sound provides no new information to the hearer. If this be really true, it may be that the drone, giving of itself no new information at a sensuous level, is preeminently suited to express that which lies beyond the world of sense perception yet upon which that constantly changing perception depends for its very point of reference. Of course, I did not think of it that way at the time. On the contrary, it had a quite different motivation. I had been privileged to experience that timeless peace that can come when the being is alert and mental processes subside, and I wanted to recapture this silence in the music. This effort may or may not have succeeded, but that is how the *Meditation for Organ* was born.

I have mentioned my quest for inspirational themes and for musical material which could clothe them, and also the cultivation of techniques which would make this possible. I would add that I never let any of these factors or the influences which went into my music lead me to excesses or to obscurantism or go against my musical instinct as final arbiter. On the contrary, I believed in the need for tradition and a common language and found myself in harmony with those who thought of tradition "not as a repetition of what has been but the reality of what endures" (Stravinsky, *The Poetics of Music*). In all this, there was one further ingredient that I felt to be essential: involvement with people who were also in their several ways inquiring into themselves and into nature, people who could seek out and try out any music that seemed relevant to our ideas. All the works I have mentioned so far were written for that small group of friends, without whom I would not have got very far, and it was only later that I elaborated them for public performance.

I remember how one work came to life in very different circumstances. In 1959 an organist I knew was promoting a series of evening concerts at his church on the Lake of Zürich, and he asked me to write a choral and orchestral work for a visiting English choir and orchestra, to be broadcast by the Swiss Radio. I chose as my theme the revelations of an eleventh-to-twelfth-century Saxon mystic, whose songs are sometimes cited in textbooks on English literature as the earliest religious poems in the vernacular. This figure, St. Godric of Finchale (ca. 1065–1170), who lived to be about 105, seems to have been a sailor until his middle age. Then, responding to an inner call, he dwelt close to nature in England in a spot that is still remote from the ways of men, and for some sixty years he lived a life of great asceticism, during which time he was favored with many visions. In four of these Godric was taught songs by divine persons who appeared to him. Using this wonderful material, both words and music, as my starting-point, I set about writing a cantata called *The Visions of St. Godric,* but for a long time I could only get as far as writing the four visionary movements. I felt that a further, purely orchestral movement was needed in the middle of the work so as to rest the voices and relieve the charged apocalyptic atmosphere. In effect, I decided on a little tone poem to be called *The Forest of Finchale,* in reference to the spot where St. Godric built his hermitage near the constant sound of a running river, living with nature and unseen presences. My idea was to portray the sounds of nature and the feeling of growing things. These, however, were not to be introduced for their own sake but in such a way as to point to a central focus. I shall say more about this in a moment.

I must first explain that the place name *Finchale* (pronounced *Finkel*) is a very ancient one, and it appears to mean the place of finches. Hence I surmised that finches would have been prominent among the birds heard by St. Godric. I knew that any direct imitation of these birds would be out of place, with their high and rather screechy sound. On the contrary, it was somehow the *idea* of finches that had to be shown as part of the manifold music of nature conceived as a song of praise. How was I to proceed? Well, I borrowed a good recording of finches and by means of suitable equipment slowed down the speed of their song and also scaled down the pitch an octave or two. From the resulting sounds I selected and transformed elements that seemed in keeping with the other musical ideas that had been accumulating for this movement and for once thereby found machines helpful in realizing a musical result. But all these materials were in a fragmentary state, and I had not yet found a form which could bring them together in a single mold. This was still the situation about ten days before the performance on the Swiss lake was actually due.

The next day, at the height of a fever, it suddenly came to me —the golden section, formulated by the ancient Greeks as a supreme canon of proportion, a canon which was later to inspire so much in European architecture, painting, and design. There was actually much in the works of the classical composers which suggested their awareness of it, too, though this may have been at a purely instinctive level. Could it, I wondered, be properly applied to music, or was it only for the plastic arts? Well, the answer to my problem seemed to lie in a related mathematical series formulated by the thirteenth-century Italian mathematician, Leonardo Fibonacci of Pisa. For in the Fibonacci series, as it came to be called, each successive pair of terms approximates the golden section more closely. Quite recently I was much interested to read Hugo Norden's *Form: the Silent Language* (1968), which relates the Fibonacci series to music as well as to other arts. Now at the time when I was preocuppied with *The Forest of Finchale,* I knew that certain creatures grew in the proportions of this series, so this was the link I had been looking for. St. Godric's Finchale just had to teem with life and the feeling of growing things. It was thus that I came to find a basis for the musical form on all levels: for the main divisions of the movement, for the subdivisions of these, for the rhythmic figuration within successive bars, and for the entry points of the various melodic themes.

When the time came around for me to leave for Switzerland, by car, the movement was largely sketched out, and I remember sitting up a couple of nights on the journey, one near Notre Dame and another at Vézelay, to complete the score. I met the soloists, chorus, and orchestra on the lake, and I remember several of us were copying the orchestral parts right up to the commencement of the first of our two short rehearsals. In *The Forest of Finchale* the intimate digest of images, techniques, and principles are all hidden under the natural sounds I imagined to have been around St. Godric in his seclusion, with his garden, the salmon leaping in his weir, the distant tune of a shepherd's pipe, and the songs of the birds. The diverse materials are united not only through the dynamic symmetry of the Fibonacci structure but also by the sounds of the river, represented this time not by a drone but by a continuously moving figure suggesting that which is always changing yet always the same, and by a suggestion of the plainchant setting of the *Te Deum Laudamus* periodically heard as a distant undertone.

There are a few last things I want to say.

I see music as an examination into the nature of the self, as a form of speculation, if you will. Insofar as music asks a question, it can only be "Who am I?" By what he understands the composer has the responsibility of conveying the highest answer that his understanding allows. Techniques and even, if necessary, the results of technologies may be helpful in making qualities of spirit manifest, and in matters of art this is surely their only proper use. As to the composer's quest for something new, it is certain to fail if he continues to put primary emphasis on techniques. Would he but turn to the spirit, he would find the spirit ever new and would see progress no longer as mere change but as the constant seeking out of materials and techniques which can clothe the spirit ever more nearly. So I believe that we have not gone beyond the point of no return, and that, if we keep this higher relationship constantly in mind, our prospects are likely to be very fair.

I believe, as Professor Needleman put it at the opening of this lecture series, that we have to find the way to live on two levels. In music I think these levels emerge as those of spirit, vision, inspiration, intuition, on the one hand; and of techniques as applied to musical materials on the other. I further believe, as a musician, that the conflicts in trying to live can only be resolved if we get the order of dependence right. For in art, as in life, ways have to be found of recognizing and attending to a whole.

Winthrop Knowlton

Winthrop Knowlton *is chief executive officer of Harper & Row, Publishers, and former Assistant Secretary for International Affairs, U.S. Department of the Treasury. An acknowledged authority in the world of finance, he is currently Chairman of the Association of American Publishers.*

THE FIRST THING you should know about me is that I am an impostor. Unlike the other speakers in this series, I am not sure I understand what "the cultural revolution" is, and I know that I have more to learn than to teach about "the art of living."

Unlike the other speakers, I am not an academician or a musician or a Zen roshi or an artist or an "expert." I am most of the time a bureaucrat, a species or subspecies that many of you may regard as part of the problem, part of the culture that makes "the art of living" so difficult.

I grew up on the North Shore of Long Island in an elegant, rural enclave, among the landed gentry. My mother and father were never really part of that world, but they wanted to be (at least my father did), and as a result of their charm and intelligence and ambition, they gave the impression that they belonged, but the effort made them deeply anxious. They were apprehensive about money and doing the right thing. Neatness and regularity (regularity of bowel movements, of church attendance, and of dinner parties had about equal billing) were the resident virtues.

I became an institutional man. I married early, embracing the institution of family. It was one of the things one did in the fifties, especially if one had older brothers who had served in the war. Almost all of them married early because they believed their days were numbered, and so those of us who were a little younger emulated them because, after all, they were heroes. About ten years later I divorced and married again. I have five children now, and as I stand here I wonder what they will say, when they are my age, about the art of living and of growing up in my family.

I quickly embraced, or was embraced by, other institutions: schools, an investment banking firm, the federal government, a publishing house, and various boards of directors. Mine has been a world of committee meetings, of minutes and agendas, of deadlines, of bottom lines, of negotiable instruments, of accountants and bankers and lawyers, of esoteric documents like 10K's, and acronymic government agencies like the FTC and the SEC. I sometimes think my life has been a pilgrimage from regularity to regulation.

For the most part, this world is hierarchal, ritualistic, and judgmental. A great deal of time is spent in problem solving and goal setting and in adjudicating disputes between conflicting interests. For those of us who have been conditioned to this kind of world, the absence of these activities does not always provide rest and relief; it (perversely) creates a sense of flatness—and, sometimes, of emptiness and despair.

These credentials do not fill me with great self-confidence standing up here before you. And *you* scare me a little, too, for you are Californians, and that means, by definition, that you have already spent a great deal of time thinking about these issues. I mean that's why you're here in San Francisco not in New York, where we are too savaged by the exigencies of daily life to speculate on, let alone *act out,* the Good Life.

And I am suspicious of talk. How much of it there is! Goethe once wrote: "We should talk less and draw more. I personally should like to renounce speech altogether and, like organic nature, communicate everything I have to say in sketches. That fig tree, this little snake, that cocoon on my window still quietly awaiting its future—all these are momentous signatures."

Well, that's a little sweet, a little charged with sentimentality for my taste, but nevertheless the point is valid: Talk is enervating, and we should be on guard against it.

Those of us who are talking together about the subject under discussion tonight represent a rather small group, I suspect, who believe they have the possibility of making choices. Why hear different views on "the art of living" if there is no possibility of trying to change, to try something new, to create the illusion of a fresh start, as though tomorrow were New Year's Day. We do not belong to that vast "other" group of people who have no choices—or at best very limited ones—because they are poor, unemployed, hungry, seriously ill, or incarcerated; or because they live in societies which permit no choice as a matter of political philosophy.

We are far more aware of all those "others" out there than we used to be before the world became so visible and accessible. Now we are acutely aware of the problems of minorities in urban ghettos, of starving millions on the Asian subcontinent, and of jailed and tortured dissidents throughout the world. These are old, old problems. They were not invented by the multinational corporation. We are aware of these "others," we sincerely care, we have choices. And yet?

Because of the repetitiousness with which the modern world is rendered (and because of the form, largely in *images*), these problems become abstract and remote. Or perhaps there is an insidious quality about our materialism and our freedom, theoretically so comforting and nourishing, that spoils and isolates us. Awareness does not always lead to feeling or to action. Like talk, it can be debilitating.

Awareness. That is really where I want to begin. Indeed, that is where I have already begun, trying to make you aware of who I am and who *we* are. Perhaps my perceptions are inaccurate—they are certainly incomplete—but at least they are mine, and for the moment you are in my hands.

Certainly one of the powerful forces with which we all have to contend—perhaps it *is* the cultural revolution—is the astonishing increase in our collective awareness of a multiplicity of problems, places, people, and things, some old, some new.

There is, to begin with, *self-*awareness. Although it is hard to believe, the self did exist before Freud: the self as individual citizen in classical Greece; the self in relationship to God in medieval times; the self as man of property in the Puritan and Victorian West. Freud and others have given us a richer vocabulary with which to speculate about the self—or ourselves—and the modern self tends not to define itself in terms of the external forces I have mentioned but by the ways in which the various *inner* selves contend and come together—if they do.

In a marvelous book called *The Adventurer,* Paul Zweig tells us that for several thousand years we have been internalizing our odysseys. Compare Homer's Ulysses, for example, with Joyce's. Today many of our journeys take place in our heads or in our nervous systems.

Of course, you could argue that this is nonsense, for men have only recently been walking on the moon.

Imagine my surprise when I was told by one of my children that the astronauts really didn't go to the moon; the whole adventure was simply a magnificently contrived television program designed to fool the Russians!

It would seem from this that even the most dramatic external adventure can today be made to feel abstract—far-off, unbelievable—both because of the delivery system that presents it to us and the power of our self-absorptions, the fierce, crying realness of ourselves, however muddled and confused the conflicting visions of our conflicting selves can be.

We are aware, today, of alternatives. Alternative political systems and lifestyles. East and West. Action and Meditation. Mind and Body. Success and Failure. Greed and Goodness. Giving and Taking. How much of everything there is at once, and how much of it before our eyes! What a mishmash of fads, gurus, dogmas, physical and intellectual and spiritual diets.

If you put the two awarenesses I have described together—*self-*awareness and awareness of *alternatives*—you can really get yourself in trouble.

For example: Several years ago I began running. I did it because several people in the office were doing it, and they enjoyed it and they said it made them feel better, mentally as well as physically. And so I started. I had already been practicing hatha yoga for a couple of years, but I missed the kind of exercise I knew from my youth, in which one worked up a real sweat (or, in today's vocabulary, "strengthened one's cardiovascular system"). So I began running a mile or so a day. One day I met George Leonard out here, and he said it would be healthier to run three miles three times a week, so I upped the ante. Then I read a book explaining that running was really a spiritual—a Zen—experience, and I learned that if I could break through a kind of "mystical wall" requiring maybe thirty or forty minutes of running of a certain intensity, I could "alter my state of consciousness." Fantastic. But two things happened as I embarked on this new adventure. I discovered from an article in the *Village Voice* entitled "Memoirs of an Ex-Jogger" that in running I was—once again—engaging in "a bourgeois, pain-is-gain mythology, an antierotic mythology, rather than a straightforward science of clean living and self-realization." In short, I was still a goal-oriented junkie. And to make matters worse, my yoga teacher informed me that if I persisted in running over city pavements, the cartilages in my knees would be so mutilated I would never be able to sit in the full lotus position again!

If I can resolve this dilemma, I think I will at last know Who I Am and What I Stand For. Or What I Run For.

We are more aware today than ever before of the *past*. There is more of it, and we know more about it. A whole book has just been written about the first five seconds of the universe; Genesis took care of the first week in only two chapters. While new knowledge of the origins of the universe and of ourselves is extraordinarily interesting, earlier visions may have provided greater solace.

Paradoxically, we are more aware, too, of the *future*.

The future is disquieting in several senses.

Many of us are more aware of it than our counterparts of the past, because we have to predict it. I don't just mean the weatherman. I mean economists, security analysts, actuaries, market researchers, doctors, real estate agents, book publishers, politicians, long-range planners. In the economic system especially—and almost all of us are imbedded in that to some extent—we have been made aware of the perils of not "thinking ahead." (Thank God we do not yet have to "feel ahead.") The buggy whip people did not think ahead. We know now that change is all about us, that our competitors are hatching new devices in their laboratories, that they are greedily eyeing market share (our market share), and so we must be eternally prepared. And for those of us whose livelihoods depend on it, this is scary, because we know we will be surprised. And we even devise plans in case there are surprises, but the surprises are always the wrong ones. *All this is very new.* In the old days, only a few seers engaged in this kind of mumbo-jumbo, and I suspect they were held in tolerant and bemused contempt. Now we have all been forced to become junior-sized versions of Hermann Kahn, and it creates great personal uneasiness. Especially since no one admits he or she is doing it. How many husbands come home and admit to their wives, "Well, today I predicted the future again, and I predicted it would come out rather well. . . . Only I don't believe a bit of it."

And then there are the broader uncertainties about the future created by our astronomers, who are the real seers. There are new words like *cosmic dust* and *black holes* and *entropy*. Entropy scares me most of all, especially as I can never completely grasp what it means. But I know it isn't good. If I lived in California, I think I would favor banning entropy before the property tax.

To conclude this list of modern awarenesses, let me add two, and they are both pictures.

There is the atomic mushroom cloud, a truly terrifying picture. My generation has been lugging that picture around for over thirty years, and in the early years any signs that we suffered from sluggishness or malaise were attributed by parents or pundits to the psychological impact of "the bomb." For many of those years I never worried about the bomb at all. But I worry about it now. There are so many weapons, so many different kinds and in so many different kinds of hands. The technology of bomb making has become so much more accessible. And we know more about the fearful ancillary problems posed by nuclear technology even in its peaceful applications. So we have a picture in our minds of possible self-annihilation. In the old days, predictions of the com-

ing of the end of the world were the stuff of religious mania—
and, in any event, the causes were presumed to be beyond man's
control. Not so anymore.

The second picture—the other most striking new image of our
lifetime—is that of the Planet Earth floating in the black sea of the
universe, the photograph taken by the astronauts on their way to
the moon (assuming they made the trip). That can be seen as a terrifying picture, too, for it shows us as small and finite and adrift in
a void and alone. But I don't think it need be seen in quite that way.

In bad moments (and there are plenty of them) these awarenesses jumble and blur in my mind and make my spirit shrivel.
One cannot do anything without somehow being aware of something else—what someone else once did or is doing or will do;
or something else happening; or everything happening at once,
in a flux so vast and formless that the only word that can give any
of it form is chaos.

How to live, how to develop an art of living in the midst of this
flux and confusion, with our heads and hearts so full of self and
the outside world?

I have for several years been haunted by an episode in a book
by Sam Keen. A writer is sitting in his room in a kind of reverie.
His typewriter is before him on the desk. He is staring out the
window. He sees a hawk alight upon a telephone wire outside.
The bird is still. The writer has no time to study its coloring or
its features. He is transfixed. He sees the bird as Bird, as though
he had never seen one before. He is powerfully connected to it.
He is lost and at the same time *joined*. He sits in what must appear
to an observer a reverie not unlike the earlier one but which,
instead, is a period of intense, pure concentration. At last he snaps
out of it, shakes his head, and reaches across for the bird guide.
He wants to find out what kind of hawk it is he has seen. At that
moment (and I cannot remember whether the author is making
this point, and if so, if he is doing so disparagingly, or whether
I have made it up) *feeling gives way to knowledge.*

I belong to a generation that was led to believe that knowledge was the key to the art of living, its centerpeice, its foun-

dation. We must learn how to learn, we were told. Our ability to do so would be tested. We would be graded. And if the grades were high enough, the gates to all kinds of pearly regions would open before us, and we would pass through the portals of Harvard and Berkeley, the Harvard Business School or Cal Tech, IBM or duPont, propelled by parents who, if they had not grown up in poverty, grew up in a state of economic and social apprehension and who, unwittingly and with enormous love, transmitted their fears to us in the form of academic apprehension. Would we ever learn or know enough? Would we ever get in? Please, dear God, let me get in. But in *where* and to what purpose?

We proceeded, as one wag has put it, as though the brain were the only erogenous zone. None of us paused to ponder Huxley's admonition that "thought is crude, matter unimaginably subtle."

The next generation reacted to this with a lot of feeling. Literally. Feeling was what they were determined to have. Looseness, warmth, openness, spontaneity, and flamboyance came in response to the relentless, goal-oriented ambitions of their parents, who in their day could have been described as knowledge children. Absolutely spent by the rigors of their ascent toward some elysian bureaucratic and suburban goal, these parents reacted to the new generation—their very own flower children—with a mixture of anger and envy.

As so often in this culture, we appear to have created for ourselves an either/or situation: knowledge vs. feeling, with related subsidiary issues generating a new vocabulary of their own; hierarchal vs. participatory; uptight vs. liberated; grey flannel vs. green anything. But the presumed conflict between knowledge and feeling was at the root of the matter.

I don't believe in these dialectics and dilemmas, these terrible choices that we invent and then let bedevil us.

When I think of the writer and the hawk, the writer turning from the transforming *felt* experience to knowledge in the form of the bird guide, I don't see one gesture or experience coming at the expense of the other. I don't, personally, see this as a progression from greater to lesser experience, from richness to flatness, from a worthy moment to something innately tired and mundane.

The transforming, mystical moment cannot be sustained. It can, however, be encouraged and nourished.

Perhaps the writer sitting in his room would not even have been aware of the hawk—would not even have seen it—if the bird guide had not been at his side, if some routinely intellectualized search for knowledge or beauty had not sensitized him to the possibility of hawks in the first place. Perhaps the discovery afterward in the bird guide of what kind of hawk this was, what name it had, was not simply the reflex action of a man processing information but a way of using knowledge to give resonance to one's memory.

Of course, knowledge too obsessively pursued *does* block feeling. Feeling too feverishly embraced forecloses knowledge. And when these things happen (and they happen all the time), the possibility of meaningful, creative action is lost. And we are left bewildered and weak by choices that have been made incoherent. And we feel guilty because we never seem to end up doing anything.

Take the academician obsessed with the accumulation of historical fact: If that's all he's obsessed by, then he is likely to become a pedant not a scholar and a teacher, which require that the subject and the student be treated with love. Take the young man or woman who wants to start a new kind of society, who is endowed with great good feelings and not much else, and who goes off to the country with his peers in a kind of utopian daze. What we get is not rural saints, not farmers, not Tassajaras, not Green Gulches, but communes in which the fences collapse and the weeds grow high.

Addressing the problem from a different perspective, Robert Pirsig wrote in *Zen and the Art of Motorcycle Maintenance:*

At present we're snowed under with an irrational expansion of blind data-gathering in the sciences because there's no rational format for any understanding of scientific creativity. At present we are also snowed under with a lot of stylishness in the arts—thin art—because there's very little assimilation or extension into underlying form. We have artists with no scientific knowledge and scientists with no artistic knowledge and both with no spiritual sense of gravity at all, and the result is not bad, it's ghastly.

While we're on this subject of lopsidedness, it is perhaps worth mentioning that there is another kind of person with no real feeling toward his fellow man and no real knowledge either. This is the kind of person who is all words and all action, all bluster and oppression. I refer to certain kinds of sheriffs in the South; urban drug peddlers in the North; certain Afrikaaners or members of the Iranian SAVAK—recurring types whose art of living involves the snuffing out of life. One can only hope they are a terrible dying breed of mutant or, failing that, that the moral acts of the truly living—those who live *truly*—will ultimately disarm them.

To return to where I was before I described the writer and the hawk:

Of course, we are confronted with a bewildering set of awarenesses in the modern world, awareness of self, of past, of future, of annihiliation, of the Planet Earth alone in the void; and in the midst of this we are made aware, by modern communication and transportation, of a boggling confusion of personal alternatives.

Of course we must make choices. Purpose is choice, and choice is painful because it entails loss. So we'd better be prepared for pain.

But life is surely more than Purpose. What of foolish or misguided or high-blown purpose? Of dogma and ideology? Surely we must find purpose that contains within it some prospect of useful fulfillment, the seeds of joy and even of good.

To find it I think we must look for those activities or ideas or situations in which knowledge and feeling fuse, and as a result of the fusion, action takes place. I am suspicious of prolonged inaction either in the service of knowledge or feeling. The writer who has "experienced" the hawk and then "identified" it must at some point return to his typewriter, not necessarily to write about hawks, but enriched, however subtly, by what has taken place.

What I am trying to say is that life is not a pendulum consisting of a relentless swing back and forth from one thing to another. Nor is it a circle, with one going round and round, always returning to the same place. Nor a triangle, with each of us hopping from one point to another—the three points being knowledge and feeling and action—but no real connections between them.

And it is not, thank you, a ladder or a staircase, to paradise or anywhere else. The closest I can come to describing what I want is a spiral, with the structural elements, knowledge and feeling, coiling up together and around each other, always close, not always touching as they should, but touching occasionally, occasionally even intersecting. There is the element of vine here and of candelabra. The action comes at the points of contact and intersection, and there sparks are emitted, bursts of energy. The whole thing looks a little like the DNA molecule or like a Fourth of July sparkler.

I am excited by this model, because it seems to me to encompass the possibilities of both change and repetition. Repetition, or routine if you will, is important, though we tend to disparage it. As Whitehead put it, "Unless society is permeated, through and through, with routine, civilization vanishes." Routines are apprenticeships; they are therapies; they are reiterations of values; they are the encircling embrace against which we measure our growth. But we would like it if the circle itself moved, if, when we returned to the old terrain, we were each time able to view it from a different angle of vision. And this the spiral enables us to do.

When I look for real models—human beings not verbal or visual abstractions—to see what actions are possible and what is right about the art of living, I look in the direction of artists. I do not mean I look necessarily at their lives. Those, as we know, can be a shambles. They cut off their ears or abandon their families to go to Tahiti or behave in other unreliable ways. Kurt Vonnegut once told a friend of mine, "We've got to get these neurotics out of the arts. They're giving us a bad name." No, I mean that *I look at the way they do their work.*

I hear Allen Wheelis describe the pianist Sviatoslav Richter come onto the stage to play with such power and intensity that there is "a passion altogether his own, a force that generates form."

I hear Edward Hopper say, "I believe that the great painters, with intellect as masters, have attempted to force this unwilling medium of paint and canvas into a record of their emotions."

I hear Charlie Chaplin, many years ago, directing his son Sydney in a play in a small Hollywood repertory theater, his voice full of enthusiasm and care. The first scene has not gone well, and Chaplin is explaining why. "This first part is everything. . . . That's why I'm dwelling on this. You must not act. You . . . must . . . not . . . act. I must sharpen you here. No self-pity. Don't give the audience the impression that you've just read the script. It's phony now. We don't talk that way. Just state it. Don't make it weary. You're too young for that. Let's get away from acting. We don't want acting. We want reality."

There is knowledge and feeling coming together. And the action? It is the teaching of one's child. It is the bestowing of gifts.

We cannot all be artists—thank God. But we can live artfully. Even bureaucrats. Even lawyers. Even bookkeepers. There is an aging bookkeeper in a Nina Bawden novel who is described thus: "She was in love, this absurd, coarse, clever old woman, with the choreography of figures: while she spoke to George about adventure capital and limited companies and merchant banks, he could see by the look in her eyes that she was mesmerized by some marvelous ballet taking place in her head."

I have colleagues like that, and so do you, who are connected and absorbed and committed.

What we have to do is take all those awarenesses I began with and *fuse* them into actions, and the actions must be gifts.

We do this best if knowledge and feeling work together, not one at the expense of the other.

We do this best if we use our sense of the past and the future to enrich the possibilities of the present. It is fashionable today to believe that we should live in the present, only in the moment. That is like sustaining the mystical trance; it is impossible. We must live in all three—past and present and future must also fuse, forming another spiral. Eliot describes it in "The Four Quartets."

And we must fuse our separate awarenesses of self and the outside world, for that is a false distinction. The outside world is "us." In a book publishing house the outside world comes pouring in over the transom every day, every hour, and we see it for what it is—the bewilderment, the vanity, the despair, the hope, and the gallantry that is *us,* trying to bestow gifts, which is what the art of living is about. That other distinction I made at the start between all of us in this room—the privileged few—and the impoverished and incarcerated "others" is a false one, too, for ultimately, in the sense of what I am describing, we are all one.

And that perhaps is the other way we should look at the picture of the Planet Earth. Instead of those fearful words I used earlier —*alone, finite, void*—perhaps we should understand that Earth is *whole*. Its surface is not a dry crust or a wall but a membrane— porous, delicate, and tough—like each of us. And it is beautiful. And from somewhere, somehow, someone, it comes as a gift.

QUESTION: You spoke of knowledge and feeling. What is the relationship of money to the art of living?

KNOWLTON: I think money is terrific because it gives you choice and time. The question is what price you pay to make it, what it does to you personally in the process, and what the alternatives are. I can't generalize that it's good or bad for everybody in the room. I think probably the accumulation of money for some people has been a source of pleasure and a kind of creative liberation and for others a kind of torment. The thing that happens to most businessmen is that they're so conditioned by the process of making money that, by the time that they've got it, they're incapable of any enjoyment from it.

QUESTION: How do we as individuals relate to government in a meaningful sort of way without feeling that we need a license or that we won't be heard?

KNOWLTON: The bigness of all these institutions, federal, state, and businesses, makes it difficult for an individual to relate to any of them. And it's not a good thing for the people who are inside those organizations, which most of us are. I would opt for smaller units. How we get from here to there politically I don't really see. I think our institutions are probably going to get bigger before they get smaller.

QUESTION: What art form has the most substance and promise for living today?

KNOWLTON: Well, a very personal response to that is that I find the performing arts and performing artists more compelling than the artists whose work is being performed. To me the most exciting and moving kind of art is chamber music and to hear four men or women playing the Beethoven Quartets with an extraordinary mixture of knowledge and feeling. There you have the small organization; there you have an action measurable and completable both for the performers and for the audience. That moves me more than, say, these paintings on the wall.

QUESTION: You said that you favored a different kind of structure, a smallness, but would you want to eliminate the suffering that is experienced by this? How did you manage when you faced this? Is the suffering to be eliminated, or is there a different attitude or relationship to the suffering that comes from this conflict between my own wish to be something and to have a meaningful life in this big structure?

KNOWLTON: Well, I have always opted for working in smaller organizations since I've left the government. I can remember going to a head-hunter after I left the government in 1968, and I felt I wanted to go to work for a small organization. And he said to me, "Mr. Knowlton, you should go work for somebody like ITT or General Motors. Big people work for big organizations, and small people work for small organizations." I think that's the attitude that we've got to do away with. My own personal response to the question was to go to work for a publishing house, which is, as these things go, quite a small institution. And within that publishing house we have tried to break it up into still smaller independent editorial units, including one out here [in California], so that we could have the kind of freshness and collegiality that comes from a really quite small group of people in touch with each other and in touch with an area and a community, therefore doing things well and enjoying it more.

QUESTION: How can you discriminate which feeling will take you in which direction on your model of the spiral?

KNOWLTON: I haven't got it worked out yet. Because I think the swirling spiral should probably be permitted to descend as well as ascend. And maybe it goes this way and that way as well as just straight up. I don't like the idea of its just going up. That reminds me too much of the goal-orientated junkie, always moving onward and upward. When I began to think of there being *other* spirals or *other* fusions, I came to the concept of the spiral by looking at the DNA molecule, which is perhaps the third most important picture that has come into our lives in the last thirty or forty years. But really if you think of time—past, present, and future—being another spiral or another fusion whirling around as with knowledge and feeling and action, maybe the compelling picture is the atom with a lot of electrons circling around a core, and perhaps you come back to the sphere rather than the spiral.

QUESTION: We want to bring the hungry and illiterate masses with us, and can we do that before they throw the earth out of balance?

KNOWLTON: Well, I share your hope. And I think that the only real hope is that the quality of knowledge and feeling on the part of enough individuals here and elsewhere is such that it leads to the kinds of moral actions and gifts that right these terrible imbalances. Those involve not only gifts in the broad and metaphorical sense but, in addition, political and institutional acts. I think that the Northern and Western world is far more sensitive to these problems than even ten years ago.

QUESTION: If man is to experience the intellect and the feeling while engaged in his work, how does he move away from the anxiety toward this other kind of motivation? You spoke about the flatness that occurs.

KNOWLTON: How does the institutional man somehow shed his anxieties so that he can get to the point where some of these fruitions take place? I don't think that one can ever shed them completely. I think that they're part of the condition whether one is institutional or not. Most of us are institutional in one way or another. It requires somehow the ability to pause and to concentrate. I think it involves taking on tasks or attempting to do jobs that aren't always too big. That may sound a little unambitious and defeatist, but I think one of the problems with institutional man is that there are always too many other people in the act, working with him, so he isn't always sure as to what it is he has done and later what he's completed. That's another reason for the smaller scale.

There are an awful lot of people of institutional responsibility who take on something quite large; they've been asked by their peer groups to do something. And they take it on and they have a momentary surge of ego-gratification. Then they have to do it. And it's a little more than they really wanted to do, but they couldn't quite resist it. Then there follows a prolonged period of fear and apprehension. Am I going to be able to do this? I wish to God I could run away from this. But you don't, because you've been trained a certain way. And the fear and the apprehension drive you on to do the job perhaps better than you would have ordinarily done it. And then there is a second moment of gratification when everybody applauds. You've not only done it, you've done it even better than they thought you would. Now they're going to let you do something else. Meanwhile, months have gone by in which you were really quite scared to death. And you'd wished you'd run away. I think once in a while you ought to be allowed to run away. And perhaps one should take on some things that are a little less ego-gratifying in the first instance and give one real continuing pleasure as one does them.

QUESTION: You mentioned a book that influenced you, one that suggested a connection between running and spiritual development. Later you found out that running wasn't good for you. What is the publisher's responsibility? Have you ever refused to publish a book because you thought it might be harmful or misleading to readers?

KNOWLTON: Several of my professional colleagues are here. We're a house who like to think we believe in quality. We do not willfully publish books containing misinformation about running or health or diets or anything else. I suppose that sometimes we make mistakes. Sometimes there are moments when we're not quite sure what we're doing. Our performance is not perfect. But our intent is to keep the quality up for our own sakes as well as for the readers.

QUESTION: You intentionally scale down your tasks in business, but in everyday life with family and children can you scale down what comes at you?

KNOWLTON: Well, I think there are situations in our personal lives when we don't have any choices. We're just trying to survive. Basic problems of health or food or shelter. But there are certainly situations analogous to business life in which we've been overambitions or unrealistic. I would think that, in marriage, the expectation that the relationship with one's wife or husband is all encompassing in one's life and the mutual obligations are so tremendously profound is something that causes a great many marriages to flounder. And if those expectations were scaled down, it might humanize the relationships, and sometimes there might be more room for imperfection. And that is an example where maybe less is sometimes more.

François Stahly

François Stahly *is internationally renowned for large-scale sculptures that blend with the environment. Although he has lectured at the University of California, Berkeley, his preference is to work like a Renaissance painter, with a small number of students living with him on his estate in the forest at Vaucluse, France. Besides "The Four Seasons," in the Golden Gateway, San Francisco, his work can be seen in the Mall at Albany, New York, and in Brazil, Switzerland, Japan, England, and his native Paris.*

A SCULPTOR HAS a kind of mission. But most of the time, I think, we miss that mission. An artist, sculptor, or painter touches something real in the world. He can touch it but is not sure that he can. Our own pretentious personalities prevent our touching what is given to us; we should be more attentive.

What is the art of living? For the French the "art of living" is a kind of epicurean way of life. It is a good life, with pleasure and not too much suffering. I am not sure that we artists can give an example of the art of living, because most of the time we are spoiled; we are very spoiled. Perhaps there is something to understand. I wouldn't say that the art of living is an art of suffering, because you cannot be an artist of suffering. One cannot be a person who is only a good automobile driver of his inner life.

The world is going quite wrong, and we are implicated in this world. We are responsible for it; we are a part of it. We have to know how to stay here and continue to work, how to accept, also to suffer all that is going on. Perhaps that is something we must learn to understand, that we have to remain in this world full of suffering people. We are responsible for them. We suffer in life, and life comes to us in a suffering way; what can we do? I think we can accept that suffering is not a thing to avoid. We can accept it, without trying to escape in suicide or drugs. There is something we can learn by suffering that is also more than an art of living.

What are artists doing today? I told you we are spoiled, spoiled in many ways because of our reputation. We cannot see clearly where we are and what we are. We are only receiving our own projection of ourselves in the world, and in fact we are cut off from the world, because there are people accepting our works as important—which is conjecture. These days artists, and especially well-known artists, are really cut off from what is going on. They are isolated by their own celebrity.

I will not be here to criticize what is going on now in art. There is something coming that is very new. Values are emerging in which the art world is not involved. Another world is coming, a world not directed by specialists in art, critics, museum directors, and art dealers. They all have been given important places in the world, deciding what is good and what is bad according to price. The young generation today rejects these values accepted for an elite and commercial purpose. A Van Gogh would not be overlooked. Museums may soon serve something higher, as people are less concerned with commercial expertise. They are looking for other values; this is what we have to learn about.

I did a very big sculpture in Paris at the University of Science. I thought I did a good work. Some students wrote, "Art is no longer necessary—don't insist." We have to learn about this. There are lots of people who don't want us. Perhaps there are other people that would be happy to have some things that we could do for them, and we don't because we are so proud of our personality. We are so proud that we have a name. We want to do something exceptional, something that will be celebrated.

We are not involved with what people need. You can do a good work for yourself, an interesting work which is a kind of monologue. But there is something we can exchange with people. Most artists think that people must come to understand them in order to learn what art is; however we have to learn what could please people and be enjoyable for them, to do some less important works without being vulgar but which could be a kind of real pleasure, a real fulfillment for people. That is much more difficult to do, because we have to abandon a part of our own pretentiousness.

I have learned that, especially in California, there are many people involved with Eastern religious problems and speculations, a kind of curiosity about whether some other reality exists; the Eastern traditions have grown up here in a very extraordinary way. Sometimes these religious questions are understood in a good way, sometimes in a very superficial way, and nobody knows where the truth is. All these people are looking for another way of life, another way of facing life. And this is a reality which will be expressed in art. When thousands and thousands of people are involved in this kind of question, this kind of seeking, it also has to come in the art world—a totally new approach. What is going on now, what is on today's stock market of art, is a quite nihilistic approach to life. We should know the difference between this and some interior conviction of art, because art is also a formal discipline, and you can do nothing without a formal discipline. It doesn't need only a feeling; it needs a special attention to what form can express and what form cannot do.

Perhaps in thirty years you will speak about Coomaraswamy, about Guénon, about Schuon, and the Bhagavad-Gita, very important things and important directions completely ignored and forgotten by specialists of the modern art world. Artists say we are involved with what is going on in the cultural revolution. We are creating exactly, we are showing the way of the new epoch, of the new age. These artists may change the world, but, no matter how sincere, they are too expensive to be trusted completely for revolutionary testimony.

Fountain, Kaiser Steel Corp.
Fontana, California.
Height: 20m.
1962.

Fountain of the Four Seasons
San Francisco, California.
Height: 6-8m.
1961-64.

Granite Fountain, Parc de Vincennes, Paris, 1967-68.

"Château de Larmes."
Height: 1.5m, Chestnut wood.
Coll. Darthea Speyer.
Paris.

"Venus" (first version).
Height: 1.2m, marble.
Museum of Modern Art, Tokyo.

"Fête." Height: 70m, bronze.
Museum of Modern Art, Sao Paulo, Brazil.

Model for a fountain.

"Combat d'oiseau." Height: 2m, bronze.
Parc de Louvecienne, near Paris, 1960.

Courtyard at the artist's community.
Crestet, Provence.

"Victoire de Tassajara," (The sun triumphs over darkness; after an Indian legend.)
Height: 2.5m, Cedar wood, 1959-61.

"L'Eté de la Forêt." Height: 8m, oak, 1964-66. Nelson Rockefeller collection.

Detail of "Hydra."
Height: 2.5m, 1968.

There is a very simple approach to art. A new possibility of art has come in my life, sharing something with other people. That is not easy, because what can we share? What kind of reality can we give to people who work with us? Some things we can do by ourselves; some things we can share. A part of our work is a work with materials, but a part of our work is something that we can only do by ourselves. Later I will show you some work that I did isolated by myself and other works done with young people that I trained. Some I did with specialists, with workers. If you have a monumental work, there is no possibility to do it by yourself. A sculptor can never do a large work by himself; he has to be helped, but how? What can be shared when he is trying to stay with his own work, and what is lost in the sharing?

I made a model of one task that had to be realized, and I supervised the work in order that it be done in good form. Other smaller works I've tried to do in a kind of collective workshop where very interesting contacts were possible with some young people. They were interested and involved in the way I worked. If you proceed in a large work, lots of things that were not done in the small model come up and decisions have to be made. In a certain moment specific things can really be done together. It is necessary that you have good relationships with these people and show them something that can be shared. This is very limited. Sometimes ordinary people work with you and feel what you intend, and you can really bring them to understand things that they have never understood. Once I had a laborer with me for setting stones. He said, "This stone, Mr. Stahly, it should be here and not there." It was very difficult to say, "No, it should be there, I am sure." But I told him, "Perhaps; we can try, we have time. The crane is already paid for for the whole day; we have an hour more, we can try these two stones here. You will see." Then I placed the stone and told him, "You see this stone here. Don't you feel that the rhythm is too simple, there is no progression of a kind of rhythm there?" He knew nothing about rhythm, but I showed him that some things had to be high and should not go in the same way, that there had to be interruptions. He said, "It's true. It's much more expressive so." For me it was an experience really shared, but this has its limits.

Are we really so alone? Am I only the one who gives direction, or is there also something that we can do together? In a certain stage we can do it, and in another we cannot. When people work together, certain of them are really with you. They are really involved with what you do, and they understand exactly what is to be done; there is a kind of community working. You don't have to say this or that; you work, and you feel that the people who help follow you in the right way. There is this fantastic unity in a small group of people. It's a kind of *cadeau,* a kind of gift in rare moments. And then it's gone, and it doesn't come the next day. This sense of community can be held for a moment, can completely galvanize a little group; afterward, when they depart, all we shared is forgotten. This is a problem that all people who supervise have to consider. There are some wonderful moments we can have together, but a creative artist always returns to his solitude. And his solitude is really the most difficult to afford, to stay with.

There is a kind of vibration that we can communicate. It's very strange. There are some moments and communications when we feel that the world is made up of elements that are communicative and that can help you and can be shared. Sri Aurobindo says somewhere, "Beyond a certain level of consciousness, vibrations take the place of ideas. We hear. There are literally waves, rhythms which take hold of those who seek. Then these vibrations are covered with words, or music, or color. If the poet repeatedly revises his poem, it is not to improve its form, as he says, or to express it better, but to capture this thing which vibrates. And if the vibration is not there, all of his magic collapses."

The most fantastic thing that we can find in art is this kind of vibration. And we spoil it all the time. When we work a long time, we come to some interior domain where these vibrations are really acting. What we are doing is no longer done by ourselves but is given. There is something that is opened by another reality, and this gives a fantastic happiness to an artist who touches this thing. He is right, in this moment. Then he grasps and tries to capture it and he is lost. The only thing that we have to do in this moment is wait, stop, be attentive, and accept that this very restful moment is a gift. We cannot manipulate the way we come to this. We cannot possess it. That fantastic element could be the real shock of an art work.

Naturally these phenomena of vibrations have been realized by artists many times through all civilizations. No cultural revolution will change the inner faculty of sensitive human beings. Certain forms of cultural revolution will contest these values; certain religious forms will be built up into fantastic theories of cosmic vibration because the patience was lacking to experiment with specific knowledge for each form of art.

It's not easy for an artist to speak of his work. It's very boring when we speak of ourselves, but that is the only thing we can speak about. Sometimes it would be much better to be silent and look at our work. Once when a good team of young people worked with me, there was one who had a lot of ideas and theories. We worked inside, and he was speaking all the time; so one of the young people said, "Here we never speak." That was all he said. And I was very astonished, because that was the first time I realized we discussed nothing. We worked together, and only in working were we understanding what we shared, a fantastic phenomenon.

These photographs are a kind of biography. It is very painful to show them, but is the only way I could say some things about art. I have divided them into several areas. The first is architecture, how I worked in relationship with modern architecture and problems of the city with art. People don't have time to like art, but they give you a commission because it is very good to do a cultural work. They give some specialist a job as supervisor, but how art works, they seldom know.

The second area of photographs are works I did once in a quarry with very simple people, and others done with colleagues that worked with me, also another work I did with an engineer.

The work for Albany, New York, where I had a very big project to do, was the first time I didn't work directly with my people. The biggest pleasure a sculptor can have is to work together with people; he works, he shows, he gives the direction, and he says, "Stop, you go too far! Now I have to place the piece myself." The Albany work was so big. We were four or six people moving like lumberjacks. It was wonderful work. The biggest privation for me was not to be able to stay and be actively engaged in this part of the work. I had to supervise, to show. My eye had to follow each one, the whole organization. Such a kind of work is not the greatest pleasure for an artist, because then he is really the man who supports the whole problem, and that's too much for an artist.

This work for Albany gave me the possibility to create a little workshop in the mountains. The work was big enough to justify our doing it by ourselves, better than giving it to timber workers. A new kind of approach, a sensitivity to each form was necessary. This workshop was a very interesting experience, because with my children, who are architects, I had the possibility to build as a contractor.

A new period began when I was helped by Parvine Curie, who is a sculptor involved in a way of sculpturing very close to me. I felt we could work together in a real way; it is never really together, but we try to be. Now we are married and have the courage to begin a new epoch in this small artists' town trying to give to this forest in southern France a kind of expression, something completely free. That we can do it is perhaps the biggest illusion!

My American experience was working in the middle of nature, giving me the freedom and idea to go to nature with sculpture. To do sculpture in nature gives a kind of new feeling to nature —nature is, in a way, completed or expressed. We had a barn in Aspen and had no wood. Some young students were anxious to work, and I told them, "Why not sculpt the barn?" We began to sculpt the barn, and this was the beginning of what I did later in Paris on the Maison de Radio. It gave me the idea. It was very interesting as an aspect of suggestion.

It would be very interesting for us to criticize each work as there are many things to see about a work of sculpture. We do many things, and when they are realized something is wrong and has to be changed. The contrast between the concrete and stone is not right. We find an expedient way to do it, but there are things we regret later. We have the ambition to do a work as well as we can, a kind of responsibility as artists. All details have to be correct, and the handwork must be skilled. Perhaps we are not modest enough to make mistakes. Sculpture has to be controlled, and the intention has to be shown. This is perhaps one way toward a harmonious life. We have in the mountains the possibility to integrate sculpture in nature; sometimes we relate it to architecture. This is the possibility that I would like to give to other artists. Parvine and I are trying to animate the whole landscape with sculpture. This is a way we can communicate with people.

I was speaking about sculpture which could give some feeling of another aspect of art, which is trying to come to a sacred expression. We can try. We are involved very closely with these problems, but how can we touch these things today? How we can find this way, a new necessity to animate a sacred form of sculpture? We have no interest in very precise forms of religion. We have to go toward the way which was indicated by such artists as Brancusi where a feeling about what is really inside a work of sculpture is possible to give and transmit.

My works which I try to introduce in nature are works that stay better outside than in a museum, like those in the forest at Crestet in southern France. We as artists are in the middle of an epoch of revolution where new values are emerging. We are going to the forest and we do some sculpture. We will be treated as aesthetes. It's another way to realize something that could never be done and could never be expressed elsewhere, a way and approach whereby sculpture could have real meaning. It would never be possible to do this in the middle of a town, but in nature you have the possibility. The surroundings give a response to what you are doing, a kind of communication, a kind of real integration of a sculpture which could dominate and which could create a new feeling for nature. This would give nature a completely new expression—an expression which it may be necessary to have there. Some sculpture seems to complete the landscape. The landscape gives a feeling to the sculpture, and the sculpture gives a feeling to the landscape. One of our purposes at Crestet is to work together with young people, creating a park in the middle of the forest where people can have a very new approach to the forest and to art, to the well-being of art.

We sculptors today must do something in relation to our time. What can we do? What is really necessary? What is our real purpose? Is it to abandon our possibility of a real form of art? Now, we are trying something in the middle of a world which is against all this, but we try. It is our way of not abandoning our mission, our real possibility of manifesting. It's not claimed that we contribute to a harmonious or better life, that we contribute to a life as it is described on the program of these lectures. We try to do something in our way, something that is given to us to express, and with all our mistakes and pretentions it may certainly be completely wrong. It would be better sometimes that all would be forgotten, and we could begin with something very simple. To abandon all we have done and to stay and to be real is perhaps much more important than only to be a sculptor. Most important is to be a human being.

I am here to answer questions that you will ask me. The one thing that I can say is we try some things, but we are not sure we are right. And this is our destiny.

QUESTION: You mentioned something very intriguing in regard to results that occur at different times, especially in relationship to students reaching rather extraordinary places in themselves. And you also mentioned sharing your sculptor's sense of rhythmic patterns in different forms.

STAHLY: You speak about patterns of rhythms. Yes. This is where we can perhaps have some control. We sometimes touch a kind of reality, and we don't know that it is real, but we feel that something is given. It has another kind of sound. This is perhaps the only control we have. Perhaps we could have another approach, but we do what we can. We haven't enough precise feelings for a real form.

QUESTION: When you move toward a work, do you have a specific content or meaning that exists in the material toward the realization of your sculpture? Is there a content and a meaning which is inherent in your move toward a work or, when the sculpture is being created, do chance incidents, accidents, occur, which also add to what you could think the meaning would be?

STAHLY: It's very interesting, your question. It's true. We don't go directly to a meaning. We are not expressing something which was there for us like an outline. We are looking for a significance which could be there. And we are building toward it with what we have inside us; we hope to touch it. Now, today, perhaps any form is possible. Each form can give you some realities. You can have a lost piece of wood, a lost piece of stone or a broken stone, and you work at it. And once you work, you are in another mind. Slowly you go toward something. It's not very clear in your mind. But you go to something you are seeking. And in a moment, you see. You see. Really it comes to you. It gives you a more precise idea of what is possible. In the multitude of forms which are offered to an artist, there is always a possibility to be real. No longer is there a reference that it should be a god, that it should be a divinity. What we have is a kind of cosmos in which we can live.

QUESTION: In your experience how can you see relationships between vibrations, or other states of being that you were just describing, input, information, or visions?

STAHLY: You speak about technology. We are in a world of technology, and we do work that is absolutely not involved with this technology, which is perhaps a lost way, but a way in which there is a possibility to realize ourselves.

QUESTION: Is that self that you are talking about operating as a source that is unpolluted or uninfluenced by all of the sheathes of experience between your expression and your discovery of vibrations? Is God or that source independent of this external experience?

STAHLY: In a way you cannot go outside yourself. You cannot go out of what you are. You are some things—you don't know what. But inside you have a kind of reference. And this reference comes when you work; it comes if you work intensively. These are references that are given to you very specially. You don't know from where and why they are given, but you touch them and you keep it. Perhaps you keep it too much.

QUESTION: Is there a process that you have found, that you would conceptualize what comes to you, so that you have something to express, a view?

STAHLY: Yes. In a certain moment there is a kind of necessity in yourself for a certain kind of work. At this moment (and I think it is the best way to go) it is necessary to be attentive to work, and to see what is going on in yourself—to be careful and not have illusions about what you are doing. There are always illusions concerning what we are doing, because we build images about what we do. What comes out is very different. And why is it different? It's a kind of secret, why it's different. It becomes different in your hands. You want to do something very smooth, and it becomes rough—or the contrary. You don't know. It's very secret. It comes partly from you, from a part of you, and then in a moment you feel you are closer to what is real, and this is a very, very special moment in the life of an artist. And he shouldn't spoil it. And we spoil it all the time.

QUESTION: You have a conception of something that you want to do, perhaps a model; then you expand that into a larger form. What happens to the vision that created the model? How do you get back to that vision? How do you retain something over such a long period of time?

STAHLY: That's a real difficulty, to keep ideas that are old and do something with them. Many times it would be better to change. That's a dramatic situation—the position of an artist with a work five years old and a new commission accepting the old form. He must go ahead with this old idea. You have to follow something which is dead in you. That is a catastrophe!

QUESTION: You mentioned in some of your sculptures you find yourself reaching for the sacred or to express something sacred. It sounds like maybe you do that in all your sculpture, but if it's only in some, do you find that approach in any way different from others?

STAHLY: This is really something that happens for every artist, that we come to some forms that are sacred. We come to these forms if we are attentive enough. Most of the time we are not attentive; so the forms disappear. This very precise moment is what we lose all the time, because we would like to keep the moment, and we cannot keep it. But we can stay with it and wait —and you will think, "I will have to begin again and destroy the work. It is nothing." Suddenly you see what to do. The miracle is that you see. You see—it's real! You see something that you have never seen. Where does it come from? I don't know.

QUESTION: I was impressed by the studios which you built— the austerity, the simplicity in which the students lived. What effect does this have? You must have done it intentionally—no windows, nothing but skylights.

STAHLY: Yes, it's a kind of convent.

QUESTION: I wonder where you consider yourself in relation- ship to Christian artistic traditions. I wonder if you see yourself as reinterpreting Christian art, if you see yourself as adding a new chapter to the artistic tradition of Christianity, or if you see the spiritual direction of your work as in some way outside the Chris- tian aesthetic tradition?

STAHLY: Today we have no tradition of sacred art, nor are we attached to a kind of human figuration of the sacred. We have no real contact with such a tradition. We lost it; it's our position. We are no longer involved with all these kinds of anthropomorphic figurations of divine expression. We have no necessity for that. But the sacred, I think, is in us, and it needs to be expressed. It needs to be expressed through us, only it is not appreciated today. It is not appreciated at all. All the art world is against the sacred. So we leave. I care nothing about this especially, but people are going this way. They are really in a new field and don't know where they are going. It's a kind of adventure, where to begin. It's our very great problem: We don't have this relationship with the figurative, anthropomorphic presentation of something sa- cred. Perhaps we could find it another way. For me the most interesting approach was by knowing Brancusi well. He had a real feeling for what is sacred and gave indications in his own works close to this direction. He was perhaps the only one in his time that did it. He was convinced of it, and his own life was directed in this way. Only he was spoiled, as any artist is spoiled by success. Sometimes he manifested the whole panorama of his being as an inspired artist.

QUESTION: I am interested in the relationship that you mentioned about the act of seeing and the dependence, the need to understand form. It seems to me there's a tendency for modern artists to go in one direction or the other—either a dependence on form or an escape solely into this miraculous event of seeing. Does bringing these two things together seem important to the idea of just living?

STAHLY: Yes, you are speaking about the relationship that our life can have to this kind of approach. Is this the question? We are leading our life. We are doing something that would not be spoiled. We try. We want to be sincere. We want to be real. And art is certainly a way to touch something real. Art is a way. It is one of the ways. There are so many ways, but it is one of those ways that are the most spoiled, because the whole art world is spoiled. Although it is most difficult, we have to find a way to go away from that art world.

Maria José Hobday

and

Douglas Auchincloss

Of Native American descent, Sister Maria José Hobday *(Order of St. Francis of Assisi), has studied architecture, engineering, and law besides being educated in literature, psychology, and theology. Working to serve the needs of American Indians in various places, most recently in Sells, Arizona, she has been especially concerned with people who need self-determination or suffer from depression.*

Douglas Auchincloss *has worked with* Time *and* Newsweek *magazines on both the editorial and management sides. He acted as assistant to the late Henry R. Luce. For sixteen years he was religion editor of* Time, *where his cover stories included such personalities as Paul Tillich, Buckminster Fuller, and astrologer Carroll Righter.*

HOBDAY: I come from a kind of fractured culture, myself. My mother was half-Seneca Iroquois and she looked like a full-blooded stereotyped image of an Indian, from the Tanawanda reservation in New York—long black hair, bright black eyes, very bronze skin, and high coloring. And my father was a quarter

Seminole; he came out of the swamp Indians of the South. I grew up in the Southwest with the Utes and the Navajos. When my mother and I would go to a restaurant, which we did only occasionally, they would not serve my mother, who was an Indian, but they would serve me, who was not. And that was always a very poignant experience for me, to have that kind of response to the half of me that looked so different. I had my dad's naturally lighter features and curly hair, and just didn't carry this image that people identify with Indians. But my mother did, and she took this with a kind of grace; I took it with a kind of anger, a sort of hostility. She responded with courtesy, and I upset milk on the table and left. We had our different ways of responding. I used to talk with my mother about these things, and she would say, "There comes a time in life when you have to understand that everything fits or nothing does. You have to embrace all of it. And if you can learn to do that, what looks powerless will become powerful, and what looks like death can become life for you, even though it's deadly."

I think that kind of attitude from my mother is what I would want to bring to life a little bit today. When I look at America as I move around this country, meeting different groups, all of whom seek vitality in a spiritual center, or a heightened awareness, or some way in to other people's lives, I find consistently this tremendous struggle (I mean that in a good sense) in the call to be simultaneously simple—that is, to work at the same time with all the pressures and the pulls and the diversities and the anxieties and still move simply and powerfully through it. There is a great power we have in our age, and that is the ability to do many things. They can be fragmented in the way we work with them, or there can be a kind of simple, central focus that we work from. And if we can get that focus, I think the art of living in a cultural revolutionary atmosphere is really not only possible but perhaps extravagantly hopeful.

AUCHINCLOSS: I agree that perhaps there are some good things about the multiform revolutionary times that we live in. One positive thing is that we are so uncomfortable with it, and the more uncomfortable we are, of course, the more awake we are. Another aspect occurs to me because I'm from what is called now the media. That is, we're living now in times of galloping show-biz. It's not even creeping anymore; it's galloping.

When I was first writing for *Time* magazine, I remember an editor taking a story of mine, calling me in, and throwing it back at me. It's a gesture that editors must perfect—that throwing of the story back at you, physically. And he said—the story was about an educational program that Harvard had undertaken— "You don't seem to realize you're an entertainer." It had never occurred to me. I thought that I was to write a story about the educational program at Harvard with all the facts in. Not so. I was supposed to do handsprings and please the crowd.

Well, this was many years ago before television, and television of course has turned everything into entertainment. We sit looking at the news in the same chairs, with the same expressions on our faces that we have later on looking at some sitcom or cops and robbers show. The news is packaged as an entertainment and presented to us by entertainers. The people who are in the news all think of themselves as actors. All the presidents and all the wheelers and movers and shakers have been tuning themselves increasingly to this entertainment role, whereas we are turning ourselves more and more into audiences. And that's the bad thing, I think. We are left watching, criticizing, not being in it ourselves, confronted by superstars all the time.

Watching a sports event, the man who is playing is the best there is. We are confronted by too much perfection; even listening to music, we are accustomed to absolutely perfect performances that have been created by the use of tape—taking a little segment here, a little segment there—and so there has come among us this dichotomy between professional and amateur. And it's too bad, because professional is a good word, amateur is a bad word. To say that it's an amateurish job is really to put it down, whereas amateur really means lover—a person who really is concerned. So I think that we are being made much too passive and much too afraid to act. The question is what we do about it.

HOBDAY: I had to smile when you were speaking of having your story thrown back at you. I had a life thrown at me in a very special way. And I think the art of living today has an awful lot to do with our consciously entering into the life that's thrown at us. I don't have a television, but I check it out occasionally to see how it's doing, and I find that observing is such a key to entering.

When I was twelve, I was waiting in the kitchen one Saturday morning for my best friend to come. Now I grew up with many brothers, and my best friend was a neighbor girl I really loved to spend time with, because I lived in such a disaster area most of the time. I was waiting for Juanita to come, and she was late, and I was just being difficult. She wasn't there, and I was getting tired of waiting and getting impatient and giving everyone in the house a difficult time. So finally my dad came to me and he said, "Jo, get in the car and take a blanket, a book, and an apple; I'm going to take you somewhere." Well, I was indignant because I had my day planned, but my father was a little more indignant and he was bigger, so I went. Daddy took me down to a canyon rim just about eight miles from home and he said, "Get out. Take your blanket, your apple, and your book. We can't stand you anymore. Stay down there all alone today till the rest of us can live with you, and I'll be back for you at six o'clock. Learn something by yourself."

Well, you know, I was furious at the nerve of him. Eight miles for me to walk home was nothing, but the thought of him when I got there was something, so I delayed a little bit. I was so angry I threw that book and blanket and apple right over the rim of the canyon, and went through a variety of things to get myself together, mostly inner cussing and quite a debate about the role of father and child, and the nerve of parents and whatever. About noon I got hungry, though, so I went over the rim and retrieved it all and dragged it back up, and spread that blanket under a piñon tree, put that book under my head, and started to eat the apple and look up.

And you talk about things just being thrown out. I got thrown out into solitude, thrown out into the land—and thrown into my own limits. For a few hours I hated him, then I thought there was probably a purpose, then the world became beautiful, then I wasn't bad either, and finally he was recovered, also, in the process. But by the time Daddy came to get me at six that night, I think I had had my first real taste of loving solitude. And I feel that the way that my life has been beautified and met, whether I'm in the middle of a city or whether I'm in the country, has been very much influenced over all of these years by Daddy throwing me out—with my bad disposition and my unwillingness to relate to other people creatively—and forcing me to learn.

So, to come back to television—we can really be muted by it, but we can also observe it in a way that can call us into participation with life. There is a little zone there you want to watch.

When you were speaking about amateur as lover, a thought came to me about the tribe that I work with, the Papago tribe. This is the second largest tribe in the country that is intact. And it is much more with its own traditions, because we've been so isolated; we extend down over the Mexican border in the desert, the Sonora desert. Marvelous country, but our people are hardly known in the United States. And it's because they're lovers. If you're fighters, you make history, you bloody up the pages, you make heroes of somebody else, at least in how they're written up. But if you're just a lover, you hardly ever get written up for it. And maybe the art of living in our culture has something to do with this whole way that we have of dealing with life—of learning how to be a lover. And yet to understand that sharp sword that you've got to have to protect and to promote what you know is a vital life source.

I feel that in our young people, and many of us are becoming more skilled and sensitive in this area. Somehow or other we have to be personally involved in converting the packages of the media into the kind of stuff that throws us not out of, but back into, life —with some sort of new personal center. To be a lover is very, very risky; that's my experience. But if you live life or you love people or you love dogs or you love underdogs, you know whoever you love. It's very, very risky. And the worst risk of all is to love yourself, because then you have to go against an awful lot of currents and suctions and stereotypes.

Like with our people. Many of our people down in the desert simply don't know how to cope in a competitive world. If you want to pick somebody to be around that's sweet, they've got power. And they're tremendously observant, because they've developed the nonverbals. One of our people can sit next to you for fifteen minutes and defend the best of your qualities for twenty years. They also recognize the other stuff but don't talk about it, because they don't talk so much. But I wonder about the real confrontations that we have to personally have with solitude, and with what our style of love is and the world that we want to love, and how the media can be a call for us to love, what it is all about, in terms of the simultaneity and simplicity and a cutting through of what can distress us so very much.

AUCHINCLOSS: What you say about spontaneity and simplicity brings me to one of the most powerful symbols that I have encountered in my long life. It's a symbol I'm sure that you all know. It's the Shiva Nataraja, Shiva dancing. You remember that he has four hands, of course. In his right hand he has a drum of creation, in the other hand a flame of destruction. In his right lower hand he's making the gesture of fear-not. With his left lower hand, he's pointing to his raised foot. And that raised foot is the key, the dancing, the foot of liberation, of freedom. In this symbol of Shiva dancing, which is very much like the lover, there is the creation of the whole universe—as dancing, as the gratuitous act, not done to make anything, not done with an eye to the future, not done out of knowledge, preparation, but right out of his being. The god is creating the dance.

And this I think has a message for us particularly nowadays. The dancer is not giving a damn about what's going to happen, how it's going to work out, about what he's making; he's just doing it. There is the creation, that is, the creative and gratuitous divine activity. I think we are confronted by all the suffering and annoyances and alienations of life, and the fear of not being able to perform adequately or superbly. If we just remember, as I occasionally do (I don't want you to think for a moment that I'm a dancer), this symbol comes to me and enables me to be engaged and not to give a damn.

HOBDAY: That reminds me a lot of the Sioux dance. If you've ever seen Sioux festival dances, the power of a good dancer is to not put his foot down if the drum doesn't beat. And that means that you have to be as quick and as sensitive at anticipating a beat that doesn't come as you are in responding to a beat that does come. So contest dancing depends on the power of the dancer to withhold putting the foot down. You know, a little like you said, when the drum doesn't beat, the power of the drummers is to keep surprising the dancers. And the skill of each is tested, one against the other. If you keep putting your foot down when there's no drum, that's distress, especially if you're contest dancing. But if you keep holding that foot, if it doesn't quite leave the air at that moment, that's called real power. And I think that this relates to a sort of simplicity that we have to come to decisions with, personally.

I try not to use the word *preach,* because I think what everyone does with life is a very personal, tremendous journey. I talk about simple living and I try to live very simply, because I live with simple people who do not have a lot of material things but many other gifts. Yet I think we can all relate out of this dance image, with a lot more dignity and reverence and respect—without knocking each other down— than we do. I've thought a lot about it; this isn't any kind of a high answer, but it's a working answer that quite a few people have tried and find works. And I try it, and it works periodically; apart from the fact that we're all basically pack rats, and all of those real things that afflict us and affect us and delight us.

It seems to me that unless we make personal decisions about what we need for creative living, we never will get into the art of living.

Now one person's need is somebody else's disaster. Isn't that kind of true? Or one person's desire will be someone else's abstinence. But I feel that you and I, when we've had enough experience about what makes us happy, what pleases us, what recreates us, what gives joy to other people when we're with them—when we get some experience in that, we need to sit down and reflect on the data, and then we have to start making choices, in the world of things. I think things are hard, because we really live in a very consumer-oriented society. I don't care how clever you are, you get hooked somewhere along the line; some of us get hooked by thinking we're not hooked—that's the basic hooking that I see going on. I just love it when people go off and live for one year apart from the whole world and accomplish it. So I think that in all of these worlds, if you say "What do I really need?" that really means psychologically, for your social awareness, for your physical well-being, for your personal development.

But there's a need world and there's an accumulation world. And I believe that we promote the art of living when there is real simplicity and basic freedom in our lives. This is one reason why I'm a Franciscan. Saint Francis of Assisi, for me in that tradition, kind of put a real human, delightful, laughing, clown touch on so many things. And if we could decide what we need, then we can do a kind of clearance, have a garage sale or an attic sale or a bonfire or go to confession —there are lots of ways to clear your territory. And, once you clear it, to really promote your own freedom by a kind of principle of replacement instead of accumulation. It has to be tested and lived with, but if you love books and you end up having to have a caravan to carry them with you throughout the country, somehow it seems to me that the very love becomes a burden and a baggage. And yet if you can say "I love books, but ordinarily one truckload is all I'll ever try to transport with me," then you already have a principle to work with; and once you can limit it to a truckload, you can get it down to a cart, and once you can get it down to a cart, you might get it into two steamer trunks. What really begins to happen is more and more you learn the books, you get them in your head and your heart and your hands and your touch and your feet, because you can't haul them around, you haul them from within. And I think that has something to do with this art. When so many things are so indefinite—one day you have social security, the next day you don't, then one day you have a job, and the next day you don't—there's something there that relates to dancing. Dancing with things. Dancing with ideas. Dancing with freedom. Knowing when to put your foot down. And when to not quite touch, because the beat's not coming for that move.

AUCHINCLOSS: You have a great sense of play. And this is a tremendously important thing for us to remember—to play. It doesn't mean that we don't work but that our attitude toward work must be the attitude of play. It's a divine attitude, it's the gratuitous god Shiva again. He's dancing as a form of self-expression. And we have to remember over and over again that we must act from our being, from our playful, loving, amateur, dancing self. That's what Saint Francis suggested to me at that particular point.

HOBDAY: I love him because he goes against sanity. I believe in being sane, but I don't know anyone who is. If you look for sanity, it leaves out so much of humanity, and it gets everybody in if you can walk on the fringe a little bit. And I think Francis was a very suffering, caring, loving, delicate, compassionate person, but he had a way of letting the bread rise; you know, once the yeast was in there, he let the bread of the moment come to life, and then you could eat that later. It didn't turn into hardtack on you, it was something you could spread with your own particular peanut butter, whatever it is, and say this is a loaf worth baking. You have to really kind of go into the future with that —we'll spread it with whatever we get, and some people might get manure at that moment. But it's got to have something, I think, for a basis that can rise and lift us into a place where our individual taste, gift, power, relish, joy for life has a chance to really become nourishment—for ourselves and for other people in the sharing.

AUCHINCLOSS: There's a thing about joy for life that makes me want to bring up another symbol that has been important to me. Once upon a long time ago I was in a park looking at some ducks swimming in a pond. And for some reason that I don't understand, I raised my hands around my eye and looked at the ducks through that little cylinder made by my hands, and suddenly they were more real than I had ever imagined. Suddenly they sprang into being for me. And at that point, an electric light bulb went on over my head, and I saw that it was the frame that did it. And not only that, but I saw that we have a frame that can do exactly the same thing for life for us, and that's our death. And that gift that we have, of being aware that we have our death, is a magnificent treasure for making the now, the presence, of the moment alive and vivid. Every once in a while, I remember about that, about my death, and it never fails to make me enjoy life much more.

I was in a taxicab a while ago, and I was late for an appointment, and there was a terrible traffic jam. I was fuming—the damn taxi driver—the light changed, and suddenly I realized that where I was going, which I was concerned about entirely, didn't exist at all. The only thing that existed at that moment was me in the taxicab. The future was only an impediment to my present. And so I suddenly was aware of being in the taxicab. And as a matter of fact, the taxi driver—one of the things I discovered when I came to myself in the taxi cab—had decorated his little cockpit like a hunk of home—I mean, he had pictures, he had things hanging, he had artificial flowers; it was just encrusted with junk. And not only that, but it smelt terrible. The thing that was interesting, though, was that in that moment of my presence there, I smelt this odor with a great deal of interest and pleasure.

Well, now, I've forgotten how I came to speak of my death from what you said, Sister.

HOBDAY: Life? I think I said life and you said death.

AUCHINCLOSS: But of course they're the same thing.

HOBDAY: You make me think of something there. I had many brothers. I have one left. I've lost both my parents. If you've had a lot of personal death in your life, one or the other thing happens to you: You either hate life, or you love it more. And when I look at what the religions of the world or what spiritual beliefs or rituals try to do, it seems to me there's always that kind of weaving history, of dealing with death and life. And if you use the word *reincarnation,* or the word *total embrace* in yin-yang, if you use the word *resurrection,* then something of what you spoke about in that little telescope of your own hands comes to life.

My personal experience is that I live better if I get into the experience of the moment and not forget it. I really feel that I hold my future with me *all* the time. Like I hold the past with me all the time; the power to remember is the power to dream. And somehow it seems to me the power to dream has a lot to do with living the now. Yet if you take a word like *passover,* how can the experience tonight, hearing or not hearing—what's the power of the experience to help me pass over into fuller living? How, through real embrace of the moment, response to the situation, how can I remember, really deepen through memory, in such a way that tomorrow when I wake up I pass over from an experience that could have been dead yesterday or an experience that could have been deadly because of what it did for me, or frighteningly deadening because of the way it immobilized me, how can I pass over from that into other people's lives with a greater heart, into other people's needs with real compassion, into other people's experiences with true understanding? It seems to me what you're saying with your little telescope is that we all have our own ways of opening a greater lens on life. I think every religious experience, and every spiritual path, tries to offer us a way to open one more lens so that we can pass over from what looks ordinary into what is not ordinary at all.

There's a scene in a novel of E.M. Forster's called *Howard's End* that I read about twenty to twenty-five years ago. It's a love scene, and the woman is trying to convert the man, because he's not living like he ought to. And so she has a kind of preachment policy toward him. And she comes to a real insight about *her* life and other people's lives—that the real way to preach is through your self-understanding. There's a passage that I think is so powerful, and it comes back to your image of the dance and my feeling about *passover* as a word; it was something like this: Connect, get things together. Stop living in fragments. Get all the beastie things in you together with all the holy things in you. Get all the everyday prose that you're walking through into the poetry of what you dream and experience through beauty, and somehow you become a new being through that.

You know, there are a lot of forces outside us, an awful lot we can't control; there's a countermovement all the time at work, even while we're working with a history that has a continuity. It seems to me that this has a lot to do with our growth and what we teach our kids and our calling each other, this power to connect, to kind of diminish the fragmentation, through experience and memory and love and some kind of fidelity of where our heart's at, so that we personally don't end up splintered and hating to be part of anything because we aren't part of anything.

AUCHINCLOSS: One of the good things about the times that we're living in is that there is a strong feeling, a strong movement, away from specialization. One of the words that we hear now is *holism, holistic,* and of course that is conveniently close to *holy.* Connecting everything and attempting to deal with the whole man, the whole universe, all the disciplines, all the disparate facts and theories and thoughts and whatever, and somehow bring them all together.

HOBDAY: I think that part of that holistic approach is the inner stance of hospitality. I don't find people inhospitable wherever I go. I've been in New York, and I find an awful lot of friendly, hospitable people there. It depends on where we meet people. And where we meet life. If you and I are fundamentally not scared of living, if we've been through a few experiences of being thrown on the rim and have survived, then we are willing to take that risk of welcoming, of inviting ideas and people and their ways and their experiences into our lives and our thoughts.

When I came today, one of the young women who works here brought me a white rose. Now I never saw her and I never heard her name, but how can you not be hospitable to the whole world of a person who will pick a white rose from her garden for a stranger and bring it in a styrofoam cup? There's hospitality calling for hospitality. She had nothing she can gain from me by bringing me a rose except communion in a world, perhaps, where communion is. We don't lay our hearts against the beat of a sunset, or of another person's token of self-gift, unless we're essentially hospitable to the world.

Hospitality is what diminishes the fear, and I feel that the art of living today really demands coming to terms with fear. People can say you're a Sister, and you're naive, you poor thing. Well, I've been held up with a gun, and all kinds of things, and I got through them. Because if you trust, once in a while you get smashed, but you have to have that freedom to live and love people, or it's a terrible world. My experience is the 3 percent is kind of terrible, but 97 percent of the people I meet *are* rose-givers, on first sight.

QUESTION: Have you found some help from the traditional Indian beliefs? You mentioned "power" and "simplicity." I wonder if you could say whether you had found something in the traditional spirit.

HOBDAY: A great deal, and I would say to every person who lives in America: Unless you study native American traditions in their purest form, you'll never learn to live on this land with very much real direction, because there's a spirit that's already alive here, and you must touch a spirit that's thousands of years stronger and deeper.

I would say that basically almost all Indian tribes that I know value hospitality over possession. Now I'd say that's a principle that you need to think about. Most native American people feel that the most difficult thing American people have to work with is something in their blood that wants more than they need, whether other people have anything or not. Greed is another word for it.

Did you hear Simon and Garfunkel's little song, "Who Would Love a Little Sparrow?" Remember that thing? It came out, "Not I, not I," said the tree. "I need all my branches for myself." And "Not I," said the wheat field. "Gee, I might starve—nothing to plant next year." "Not I," said the swan. "What'll they think if they see me with a sparrow?" You know, these kinds of things come through. So I say, basically hospitality over possessing yourself—possessing with others rather than self-possessing, walking with the dead.

I don't know how you really live into the future happily yourself if you don't remember the dead, because you know that if you don't walk with the dead, love those whose life flows in you, who nourished your ideas, whether it's Shakespeare or Sophocles or your mom, why you know you're doomed to be forgotten unless you can remember yourself. Does that make sense? So I would say that would be another principle.

Another principle would be silence, a tremendous respect for anyone who can keep still and still communicate, a tremendous respect for anybody who can live in the midst of sound and not have to have noise overwhelming it—sit with the wind and not have to turn on the transistor to drown it out, because it's scary when you sit with the wind.

I would say, too, we need a real sense of harmony with the land: If you can harmonize with a tree, you can harmonize with a man. If you can harmonize with a man, you've got the power to harmonize with a rock. If you've got the power to harmonize with a rock and a tree, you'll understand natural resources differently than if you've got no harmony power.

So, silence, and the dead, and hospitality, and also the sense of beat—the beat of life comes out of the earth, and out of the earth I have to do my dance. In relation to you, if I insist on dancing and you don't have room to dance, it's selfish. And if you insist on dancing and you won't make any room for me, the same, so that's courtesy and hospitality again.

QUESTION: I'd like to hear some of your views on human suffering.

HOBDAY: Well, what I know about suffering is from having suffered. You too? The rest of it, I think, sits in a textbook. I would simply say that, as I look around life, and as I pet dogs, and as I trim my little parsleys to make them grow for my soups and things, I experience pain. Haven't you had pain and nobody met it, and you learned something about yourself? I mean you either go up or you go down. And haven't you through that found that you either do or don't do something differently the next time you meet people? I think that pain is very related to a kind of tuning up of the instrument of response to self through self-discovery and response to the rest of the people by what we've experienced.

AUCHINCLOSS: One of the slogans among the Zen Buddhists, who, as we all know, spend a lot of time sitting, is "No pain, no gain." The legs have to hurt.

HOBDAY: Something has to yield if someone else gets to take. Everything suffers, from little broken puppy legs to a man who has experienced the death of his wife, to a woman who has experienced the death of a possibility. My experience of life is everyone knows pain. And I know a man who knows pain because he doesn't think he knows pain. He worries because he has never experienced the pain of other people. He always got to ride when they had to walk. His pain is really pain.

But it seems to me that the experience of observation and personal participation in life is that pain and suffering are what you embrace if you embrace life, and my experience also is it'll make you or break you. I know people that come out of it believing and loving and giving and helping and doing. I know people that come out of it hating and bitter and withdrawn. But I don't know anybody that stays in one state forever.

It seems to me that even if I could come out of a certain experience—and you know how we can come out sometimes if we have really been put upon—there's nobody that hasn't been mistreated, or diagnosed, or put aside, or stereotyped, or castigated, or castrated, or something by someone, so my own experience of that tells me that we all somehow have to make those decisions of embrace. And sometimes we can't; we're so psychically beaten, so physically sick, we're so terribly abandoned that we just come through it with a lot of pain. But I feel that it's the passover. I think that most people I know who touch tenderly and gently are people who have been bruised. Most people I know who learn how to look with welcome and affection and hospitality are people who have had a look that kills from enough people that they don't want to inflict it on someone else.

I see suffering as an inseparable part of life. I can't put it to my own satisfaction into terms that are analytical and defined, but I know it, I experience it, and I find a lot of good fruits in it. Ultimately many people are broken only to come back to life, after having been shattered. Other people just go through life with cracks all the time. You know, we live differently. Some people, it seems to me, are just always hurting but never aching. Other people are falling apart, and they don't understand these people that don't walk with perpetual headaches. But if we can keep open to each other, our worlds flow in and out.

I know people who I think have as much pain because they can't solve for themselves what we should do with the atom as people who have pain because they don't know what to do with their kids. And you don't do anything, ultimately, with kids; they're free beings, too. Bury 'em and dig 'em up twenty-five years later to see what happens. But the pain of twenty-five years of waiting for lives to form, to take shape, to come to meaning and creation I think makes us a certain kind of people, and what that is is very mysterious. Pain is very mysterious to me. How about your experience there, Doug?

AUCHINCLOSS: I agree with you that it is mysterious, and that it's necessary. And the other great religions don't emphasize that so much as Christianity does.

HOBDAY: I feel that Christianity is from the West in a special sense, and we're embracers and doers. I love so much of the Eastern tradition, but I'm not very passive in style; I'll go do it instead of letting it get done to me, and most Americans I know are of the same cut; we're cut from that kind of cloth.

Why is it that there is such a tremendous difference in that approach? I think the Eastern approach is something that as Americans we need to really learn, because our endurance level is so low. Our tolerance for pain is so irritable; I mean, we get aggravated. And yet part of life, it seems to me, is that at certain times for greatness of soul, for magnanimity, we are called to bear, and at other times we are called to wrestle. And I think the Western world can teach the whole world a lot about wrestling, but we get so agressive and bicepty with that principle that we better get in there and learn to sit down and take it sometimes, because that's all there is to it anyway that promotes peace.

QUESTION: I read that you work with depression, and I was very interested in that, especially in all the marvelous qualities that you have been showing us and the vast gap between that and the state of depression.

HOBDAY: Well, I think we all experience depression, and if you don't know you experience it, then you need to know you experience moments of depression. They may be very fleeting or passing moments like self-doubt or self-worthlessness, an experience of sadness you can't account for, a momentary loss of hope, those kind of pits that we hit. If we will develop a kind of inner stillness—out of the Eastern mentality we get a kind of clue there

—we'll be in touch with those moments and we'll be able, when they're fleeting, to sort of meet them and smile them away. You've got to embrace them to have any power over them. It seems to me you have to embrace them.

Over the long haul one of the best ways to work with depression is through your personal dreams. And I don't mean at night. I mean your own ideals. At times when things seem to go bad one thing that we have to keep doing is remembering—the power to remember is a great power—remember our ideals and remember our friends. Remember who loves us, not so much whom we love but who loves us, who will put up with us no matter what.

Feeling sorry for yourself for a moment is very different from a lot of wallowing in self-pity. So I think the best thing to do is to let those little moments come out in front and handle them. When it's something a little larger, admit it if you can.

Sometimes I have to pray. I simply have to go deep and say, wait a minute, what am I all about, and what's my life about? Who do you think you are, trying to sidestep everything? Work! Go through it, live with it for a few hours. Try to enter in and sort of let that be a bond of understanding. Love toward other people would be another way.

Sometimes I simply have to distract myself, go look in the mirror and say, "That's right, honey, you are depressed. You look depressed. I think we ought to have a treat." That depends on where you are, what your treat can be. My favorite treat is a good cup of coffee with sugar in it, take my shoes off and lock the door. That's really good and indulgent, especially if someone knocks and I don't answer. You have to see what you're doing; you're laughing your way right out of it. So the biggest thing is to find a way for relief.

You might want to look for why you're depressed. I really feel that it's sometimes anger against other people. Many people are tired because people expect so much of them. I think depression can be very complex. Today we're living in a very complex society, and a lot of stuff is hitting us, and you may have one thing that you resent or one area that you've buried while you're involved in four other things, and you don't even realize it. Well, maybe it's at those quiet times that you surface it. I'm always worse off if I don't get quiet times, because then I don't let things surface; and if it doesn't surface, I don't face it. And if I don't face it, I lie to myself; and when I lie to myself, it's messy. And that's where I find a lot of those things originate.

QUESTION: Would you say something about working with children? One of the things that interests me is that you are the only speaker in this series who has been able to refer to your parents as people who have contributed to your art of living.

HOBDAY: My parents didn't have any children for the first six or seven years of their marriage, and my mom and dad often said to us that that helped them be better parents. But still they did have children, so I would say it's very important, if you are a life-giving, nuturing person, to not deny children a chance to receive that or yourself a chance to foster it, whether they're your children or someone else's.

I work with so many children; in certain areas of the country there are lots of kids blooming. On the reservation they're growing like little flowers all over, but across the country we're at zero population growth. I think that part of that is the change of the decades in attitudes toward children. But we don't want to ever disassociate ourselves from that truth of child, that we're all kids, and that means little people, capable of life and gifts. So whatever our personal attitudes are about pregnancy and abortion and full-term and foster children and how you parent, we've got to really get our heads screwed on a little better from a stance of love. Our kids belong to all the people. And all the people are in some way responsible for every child, whether they give that child physical birth or tax money or whatever it is.

Somehow or other we're hooked up together in life. That's what we're all about here. Let me just give you one example. I lived with a young girl once, and she handled things like a Zen artist. She touched things with so much reverence that she was a living meditation. I really was inspired by her; she really called me to consciousness. And one day I said to her, "Janet, I consider you such a gift. Just from the way you touch things you make me more aware of the way I touch everything, including my own body." I think it's tremendously important how we touch the closest physical expression we have of ourselves, our own child, which is the body that has grown. And she said to me, "Well, Sister, it's no virtue, let me tell you. I had parents that banged everything about, all through life. My mother never closed a drawer; she slammed it. She never set the table; she dropped the dishes on it. I determined to be the opposite." So what I'm saying is, we have come out of something in our kidhood that has influenced us to imitate it, change it, redirect it, deny it, or to do the opposite. And I think it's very important that we do that, and then with your own children, or with other people's children, to try to find what inspires.

In my grade school I had two terrific teachers. One magnificent, the other great, and the rest were pretty floppy as far as I was concerned. Thank God I had a mom and dad that made up for it.

My second-grade teacher influenced my life decision. I never saw a nun; I never grew up near nuns. But I grew up with this great educator, and I decided to go out and do something with people, because it was magnificent what happened to us kids around her. And my eighth-grade teacher was just the opposite. Interestingly, out of those two classes, eighty kids to a classroom, sixty of us went into education. Isn't that amazing?

I never met a good high school teacher. They were all nice people, but they were terrible teachers, for the most part. Maybe that's not your experience. I met great college professors. And they came in and turned my direction around. So I think I was being parented all the way through there. But my child experiences were the ones that made a difference.

I stole a candy bar once when I was a little girl. And the woman who caught me was one of my best teachers. There were a hundred ways she could have handled me for stealing a two-cent Ladyfinger. But she handled me well. And she educated me into a different approach.

AUCHINCLOSS: How did she handle you?

HOBDAY: She knew me, and when I came to the counter to pay for the other things and I slipped the candy bar in my pocket, she said, "Is this all you wanted to pay for?" That was my first suspicion, but I was a courageous little kid at seven, and I said,

"Yes, that's all." She said, "What about the candy bar I saw you take?" I said, "What candy bar?" She said, "Shall I frisk you now, or shall we just simply say you tried it, and it didn't work? Now, what did you really do it for?" And I said, "I was experimenting; I wanted to see if I could get away with it." She said, "What happened?" I said, "I didn't." She said, "What did you learn?" I said, "That's it. Are you going to tell my folks?" And she said, "No, I'm not going to tell your folks, because you're going to live your own life, honey. But, really, how did you feel worrying about the candy bar?" And that was the education. What happened to me inside at the feeling level is what she touched, so I said, "I was scared I'd be caught." She said, "Now, take the candy bar." And I said, "I don't want it." She said, "Take it, take it, go take it." And so I did, and I threw it away as soon as I got on a back lot. Because I couldn't eat it.

But, you know, when you ask about children, I think everyone has this stuff to draw on, and the biggest education is helping each other pull it out, look at it, and make it fruitful.

I'm terribly concerned about children, looking at them on streets and looking at them behind bars, where I've dealt with them a lot. And trying to find those different levels of what happened in our lives. And every single person here ought to be in jail, if everything were known. Isn't that true, you sinners? You're just a pack of disobeyers of the law, and me, too! What happens when you get caught and have a backup system of family or friends, and what happens when you get caught and have no backup system? Its a big world, and we have to really tune in there.

QUESTION: Is learning the art of living just learning to rearrange our environment? Because I have a kind of fantasy, and I know it's a fantasy, that we have a lot of misused material things, and we're doing a lot of things to our environment that are very much not good; and that there are vestiges of other people out there somewhere who live differently, who are fading out, who have all these things that we may have had about a thousand years ago. And on one level I know that that's not true, and at another level I feel maybe it is. So where does reality come into that?

HOBDAY: The way that we come at that I think is out of our dialogue. The way you get a handle for integration has to come out of human relationships with each other. Now the Indian tribes that I've worked with, that are being done in or are dying or will soon disappear, have been decimated by human relationships, basically. While you were having your drought, my people were praying for you. And we were living on less water than you've ever seen. My people were praying for the people in California to not be too hurt by their lack of water, because they discovered they had more than what we have in abundance. Things get very relative. So if people can come in and share what for them is abundance, when you are in a time of the stress of lack, right there is a meeting place.

I think it's big, and I think it's long-range. And aren't we awfully impatient that it happen all at once? See, it takes time. The people I live with are very fragmented right now, because they know they have superior values—moral, human, land values. And they don't know how to make a living with them in this society. And I know people who are making a good living in this society, and it's an empty living, because they've got no value system that seems to bring meaning to the heart. Now somehow or other we've got to start hooking up; the exchange is there; we're plugged in wrong, it seems to me. If you've ever worked a PBX board, the lights can all be on and nobody's meeting, because you haven't got people plugged in right. Sometimes we plug other people in, and sometimes they plug us in. And history's got to be one of the big plugs that a lot of us are missing. If we go around talking off the tops of our heads with no historical awareness, we're really hideous, if we've got a brain.

QUESTION: If somebody's interested in learning about living in this society, is it not true in your experience that some of the pains that people endure are mostly connected to the vibrations released from machinery, electronics, neon, concrete, asphalt, and mechanical devices that are everywhere vibrating at us? Don't you find that the experience of embracing that pain frequently lacks meaning? Is there any way to go through that and derive meaning?

HOBDAY: I feel that one way we learn from it, grow from it, is through the contrast it forces us to begin to produce and create for other people. Another thing I think it causes us to do is to really look creatively at the possibility for diminishing the bombardment without always giving up the good. Most people I know hate air noise, but I hardly know anybody that doesn't appreciate a plane if they have to get somewhere fast. And I doubt that there is anybody here who hasn't flown even though you hate the noise and worry about the fuel consumption. I find myself in that situation. Yet I wonder if I create enough options for myself to see how I can counteract the vibrations personally by the way I drive, by the way I am part of the passengers on the plane, by the way I respond to the people living in the slums.

I think the big thing is how many alternatives and options can you provide so that your feet, so that your foot, doesn't quit feeling just because you walk on concrete. Walk on grass meditatively often enough to know what happens. I know some people who walk more tenderly on concrete than people who walk on grass. When you walk on grass, you are dealing with a very living thing, and all you have to do is step too hard and you've bruised it beyond its ever bouncing back. We can go through people that way. Like the vibes. Some people walk through the day, and they mow everything down. Everybody's feelings, attitudes, interests, good ideas, creativity; they throw cold water on anything that's exciting. And they do that just as totally and create as many bad vibes as I think we get from a blaring television. I don't know how you feel about that, but I think that is a really touchy area to work with, but it takes a lot of thought and creativity.

QUESTION: It's refreshing to hear something alternative for a change. We can all look around, we can listen, we can read and find all the terrible things that are happening in this world, and we hear a good many people who are forecasting even more and more. I'm beginning to wonder whether many of these things are completely too large for us, whether there is any possibility that even on an individual level there is much we can do. Maybe everything has to go all rotten so that something new can be born. I wonder if you have thought about that aspect.

HOBDAY: I think that this world is groaning into something fresh and new, and I hurt at the bloodshed that is feeding it just as I think you do. But there has been a lot of bloodshed that has seeded a lot of the good that has come and gone. If you can get a world view that is bigger than we are, I don't think it is too big for us, and if it is, you have to choose right there. Do you want to go out with a whimper or a bang? Eliot says you can go out like hollow men echoing your own whimpers, or you can go out with such an embrace that the bang releases some energy, and something new and fresh happens.

I don't think we will do it alone, but sometimes I am in groups of people and watch the most exciting things happen with a hundred people that never saw each other, and yet three hours later they go out and there is energy and dynamism and hope and a sense of future that came out of this. And these aren't people so-called religious. These are people so angry at the world that they would throw a bomb at somebody if they could figure out how to make one. And yet something can happen when you get in there and you have some people working toward a possibility. Other people will lay their frustrations in the path of a new possibility, because we all have the frustrations. You can get five hundred people, and there is a kind of way they flow up and out, and you experience them as a hospitable bunch; I've been in groups, not very often toward me, where it was not hospitality and friends but it was hostility. And those vibrations come through.

I feel these are real things we take our clues from in creating a new way of living. I don't think it's going to be so strange to discover ourselves in a whole new consciousness.

QUESTION: Do you have any thoughts about the relationship of a community such as I'm assuming you belong to—you have at least two communities, you have your order and you have the tribe you're with—and the kinds of reminders that will bring it back when the sense of it is dimmed? It seems to me that in our culture today the ideas are all around us—we hear someone speak, and we're very taken by what we hear—but it so often doesn't go further than that.

HOBDAY: I think about it as a three-ring circus. All of us have some community that's akin to the bedroom, something of intimacy, something of closeness. The someones or the someone that we can identify as a place to come home to in our own hearts. My intimate community is not my Sisters of St. Francis Community. It's too big for that kind of intimacy. It's my brother that's left and my very close personal friends—like a half a dozen. For a real intimacy where I can say anything or let it all hang out or touch the spirit, or whatever. That's my bedroom, and that also relates to my prayer life with God. You're where you are, and that's where I am; that's part of my bedroom.

Then I would say the people you sit down with around the kitchen table—you know, you have a "coffee klatch". They want to borrow your sugar, and you say, "You can have my sugar if I can have a little cream." It's that world of the workaday, the meet-a-day world.

And then we all have the open road. And that's the world you have to go out into, the community of making a living, the community of working your way through life, the academic community, the office community. And in coming and going to that you meet all the little communities.

And then if I were to give you one more image—I love images because I remember the stories better—I'd take Thoreau's. I have three chairs in my cabin: One for solitude, two for friendship, and three for society. And I'd say there are times when you must have solitude, and you should not invite friends and society in until your own heart's clear. There are times when it may be a known friend or a person who needs friends, and you will sit with a certain amount of closeness and be with and for the other. And there are other times like tonight when you are in a situation where you have to welcome in strangers, people's questions, the big world you're trying to get into, and an arena that can change your life.

Now how do you remember it? Some people never remember except by forgetting. I think the greatest presence that some people feel is through absence. We say to these people "You never know what you have until you've lost it." This is the hardest way of all, but I think it happens in some people's lives.

Another thing is solitude. You've simply got to sit down and give your heart a chance to unfold and let the things that are deepest in you come up and get in front of you. I don't think you can do it without personal silence every day. I don't know of anybody who does it without that. Now some people don't look like they have any silence, and they do. Some people look like they have a lot of it, and they've got none. You can tell it because of the way the rest of the day goes. What looks like solitude may turn out to be an isolation pattern. Solitude is fertile.